CHARMING SMALL HOTEL GUIDES

Venice

& North-East Italy

GW00481857

CHARMING SMALL HOTEL GUIDES

Venice

& North-East Italy

Edited by

Fiona Duncan and Leonie Glass

DUNCAN PETERSEN

HUNTER
PUBLISHING

Conceived, designed and produced by
Duncan Petersen Publishing Ltd

Editorial Director	Andrew Duncan
Production Editor	Nicola Davies
Art Director	Mel Petersen
Designers	Christopher Foley
	Beverley Stewart
Maps	Christopher Foley

This new edition published 1999 by
Duncan Petersen Publishing Ltd,
31 Ceylon Road, London W14 0PY

Sales representation and distribution in the UK and Ireland by
Portfolio Books
Unit 1C, West Ealing Business Centre
Alexandria Road
London W13 0NJ
Tel: 0181 579 7748

ISBN 1 872576 91 5

A CIP catalogue record for this book is available
from the British Library

AND

Published in the USA by
Hunter Publishing Inc.,
130 Campus Drive, Edison, N.J. 08818.
Tel (732) 225 1900 Fax (732) 417 0482

ISBN 1-55650-897-2

Typeset by Duncan Petersen Publishing Ltd
Printed by G. Canale & Co SpA, Turin

Contents

Introduction

This is the second Italian regional guide in Duncan Petersen's *Charming Small Hotel Guides* series. It follows the success of the first, *Tuscany & Umbria*.

That book, we have learned from readers' letters, appealed especially to enthusiasts who are regular visitors to Italy. They appreciate its in-depth approach, providing many new ideas for places to stay which for reasons of space our long-established all-Italy guide cannot supply.

This guide offers the same in-depth approach: it is no mere rehash of the all-Italy guide, but contains a wealth of new entries; some are new discoveries, never published before. They include not just hotels, from humble to luxurious, but also guest houses (*pensioni*), farmhouse bed-and-breakfasts (*agriturismo*) and self-catering accommodation that has our special qualities of character and charm.

If you already know Venice and North-East Italy, and are revisiting, this guide will refuel your enthusiasm. If you are going for the first time, it is essential reading.

Venice and North-East Italy for the traveller

Venice hardly needs any introduction, famed as it is throughout the world as a city of incomparable beauty, romance and artistic wealth. Built on mudbanks which extend into the tidal waters of the Adriatic where East meets West, Venice was once a great maritime power ruled by its doges, and a place of plot, intrigue and decadence. A city of water and of light, with an atmosphere which is at once fascinating and disturbing, its fragile fabric of canals and *palazzi,* churches, alleyways and *campi* has somehow survived the threats of both flood and mass tourism, and remarkably little has changed throughout the centuries. Nowhere in Venice will you see an ugly sight; even the Macdonalds near the Rialto is just about bearable. At any time of the year you can escape the crowds of tourists who throng Piazza San Marco, the Rialto and the main thoroughfare between the two by simply slipping into the backstreets where there is always a church, a canal, a café to divert you; the best time to visit, however, is in spring and early summer or autumn, when the crowds are thinner and the weather can be lovely. There can often be long spells of warm weather and blue skies in March, while June can be wet and overcast.

Stretching inland from Venice in a great arc as far as the Austrian border to the north and the shores of Lake Garda to the west is the province of Veneto. While the landscape of the vast Veneto Plain which fans out behind Venice is largely industrialized and pancake flat (save for the green Euganean Hills and Berici Mountains), it is full of interest. The great cities of Padua, Treviso, Vicenza and Verona are time-consuming enough, but then there are the villas of Palladio and other attractions such as the charming little towns of Asolo and Montagnana. To the west of Venice, the Plain edges into the province of Friuli-Venezia Giulia, curving round the

Introduction

coastline towards Trieste and the border with Slovenia and, to the north, reaching into the high Alps and the border with Austria.

The presence of the mountains gives this guide a rich flavour and makes the range of accommodation contained in it, from Venetian *palazzo* to Tyrolean chalet, wonderfully varied. The mainly mountainous province of Trentino-Alto Adige, which stretches north from Lake Garda, feels a million miles away from Venice. As the mountains rise towards the Austrian border, so the distinction between the two countries becomes blurred. Here in this northernmost region of Italy, also known as Southern Tyrol, you will find that the people are German-speaking (all the place names have both German and Italian translations) and that they share the same culture and traditions as their neighbours over the border. The hospitality is warm, the scenery is breathtakingly beautiful, often with the jagged peaks of the Dolomites serving as a dramatic backdrop. In winter you can ski and in summer you can walk. It would be hard to imagine a more delightful and varied holiday than to start in the Southern Tyrol, descend to the serene shores of Lake Garda (in this guide we include the western shore which falls into the province of Lombardia), then cut across the Veneto Plain taking in Verona, Vicenza, Padua, and finally reach the greatest glory of all, Venice itself. You will not lack for lovely places to stay along the way, and with this guide you can plan the perfect trip.

Our criteria
Although this guide covers a much smaller territory than the majority of guides in the series, the selection criteria remains the same. We aim to include only those places that are in some way captivating, with a distinctive personality, and which offer a truly personal service. In Venice especially we wanted to give as broad a range of recommendations as possible, to suit all budgets, as hotels are often fully booked and you may need several alternatives to your first choice, especially if travelling at short notice. We found many hotels here which easily attain our very high standards; but there are a significant number, which, though basically recommendable, for one reason or another fall short of our ideal. The descriptions of each hotel make this distinction clear. Be assured that all the hotels in the guide are, one way or another, true to the concept of the charming small hotel, and that they are the pick of the dozens of small hotels in Venice. If you find any more, please let us know (see page 32).

In making our selection, we have been careful to bear in mind the many different requirements of our readers. Some will be backpackers; others will be millionaires; the vast majority will fall between the two. They all have in common their preference for a small, intimate hotel rather than a large anonymous one. Whether the hotel be a one-star hostel or a four-star *palazzo*, it has been included because it fulfils our crieria.

Charming and small

Ideally the hotel will have less than 30 bedrooms; but this is not a rigid requirement – many hotels with more than 30 bedrooms feel much smaller, and you will find such places in this guide. We attach more importance to size than other guides because we think that unless a hotel is small, it cannot give a genuinely personal welcome, or make you feel like an individual, rather than just a guest. Unlike other guides, we often rule out places that have great qualities, but are nonetheless no more nor less than – hotels. Our hotels are all special in some way.

We think that we have a much clearer idea than other guides of what is special and what is not; and we think we apply these criteria more consistently than other guides because we are a small and personally managed company rather than a bureaucracy. We have a small team of like-minded inspectors, thoroughly rehearsed in recognizing what we want. While we very much appreciate readers' reports – see below – they are not our main source of information.

So what exactly do we look for?
- A calm, attractive setting in an interesting and picturesque position.
- A building that is either handsome or interesting or historic, or at least with a distinct character.
- Bedrooms which are well proportioned with as much character as the public rooms below.
- Ideally, we look for adequate space, but on a human scale: we don't go for places that rely on grandeur, or that have pretensions that could intimidate.
- Decorations must be harmonious and in good taste, and the furnishings and facilities comfortable and well maintained. We like to see interesting antique furniture that is there because it can be used, not simply revered.
- The proprietors and staff need to be dedicated and thoughtful, offering a personal welcome, *without being intrusive*. The guest needs to feel like an individual.

Whole-page entries

We rarely see all these qualities together in one place; but our warmest recommendations – whole page, with photograph – usually lack only one or two of these qualities.

Half-page entries

Don't, however, ignore our half-page entries. They are very useful addresses, and all are charming hotels. You can't have stars on every page.

Introduction

No fear or favour

Unlike many guides, there is no payment for inclusion. The selection is made *entirely* independently.

Choosing your room

In Venice, you can enormously enhance the quality of your accommodation by securing a good room. Many of the hotels in this guide have rooms which are similar in both price and quality, but others, whilst remaining the same in price, are much more varied in quality. You can quite easily find yourself paying the same rate for a dull box as for a light and airy space with a balcony overlooking a canal, and unless you specifically ask (and make your booking in plenty of time) you are not likely to secure one of the few good rooms. Hoteliers have told us of guests who, on their return visit, ask for the room they had before, not realizing that there are far better ones to be had at the same price. Where appropriate, therefore, we have taken pains to point out which are the rooms you should try for first; in a few cases, we have advised not choosing that hotel at all unless you can secure a particular room. We have not always mentioned room numbers, as these are prone to change.

Hotels, villas, *locande, agriturismo*

The range of accommodation on offer in Venice and North-East Italy should be enough to satisfy all tastes and most pockets, with a variety of names almost as numerous as those describing types of pasta. 'Hotel' is common enough, but so is its Italian equivalent *'albergo'*. *'Villa'* can apply either to a town or country hotel and is used by proprietors with some latitude: occasionally one wonders why a nondescript town house or farmhouse should be called a *villa* while a more elegant building restricts itself to *albergo*. *'Palazzo'* and *'pensione'* generally refer to urban accommodation while *'agriturismo'* means farmhouse bed-and-breakfast, or indeed, self-catering apartments. *'Residence'*, *'relais'*, *'locanda'*, *'castello'* and *'fattoria'* are also found.

The variety that one finds under these various names is extraordinary, from world-ranking luxury hotels to relatively simple guest houses.

Tourist information

The tourist information offices for each province are listed with the relevant maps on pages 15–31. Most cities and a few popular towns also have their own tourist offices offering information on local travel, museums, galleries and festivals.

We list on page 10 Italy's official public holidays when banks and shops are shut and levels of public transport reduced. In North-East Italy, like the rest of the country, each town has its own local holiday, usually the feast day of the patron saint, often celebrated with a fair or fireworks. Venice, of course, stages its annual pre-Lent Carnival and many other events unique to the city, most famous of which are the Biennale, the world's largest contemporary art exhibition which takes place from June to September in odd-numbered years, and the International Film Festival, held on the Lido in early September every year.

New Year's Day (*Capodanno*) Jan 1; Epiphany (*Epifania*) Jan 6; Good Friday (*Venerdì Santo*); Easter Sunday (*Pasqua*); Easter Monday (*Pasquetta*); Liberation Day (*Liberazione*) April 25; May Day (*Festa del Lavoro*) May 1; Assumption of the Virgin (*Ferragosto*) Aug 15; All Saints' Day (*Ognissanti*) Nov 1; Immaculate Conception (*Immacolata Concezione*) Dec 8; Christmas Day (*Natale*) Dec 25; St Stephen's Day (*Santo Stefano*) Dec 26.

Flights
The principal airport for the region is Venice Marco Polo, and there are also small airports at Treviso and Verona which receive limited flights from abroad. Car hire is available at all three.

Orient Express
A very special way of reaching Venice. See page 164 for a description of the journey.

Pet likes
These are some of the things that stand out for us in many of the hotels in which we stayed. Maybe they will strike you too.

- Wonderful old buildings, sympathetically restored – *palazzi* in Venice, classical villas in the Veneto, castles in the foothills of the Alps, Tyrolean chalets in the mountains
- Hotels in superb positions with glorious views
- Murano glass chandeliers (pretty ones)
- Venetian marble floors (when strewn with rugs)
- Silk damask furnishing fabric (when not overdone)
- 'Buffet' breakfasts with fruit, cheese, cold meats and yogurts
- Spotlessly clean bedrooms and bathrooms – especially high quality in the mountain hotels
- Good quality linen and comfortable pillows

Pet hates
If Venetian hoteliers have a fault, it is that they are happy for their hotels to coast along rather than strive for perfection. This is for the simple reason that they have a captive audience, a constant influx of tourists who keep occupancy rates at a consistently high level. And prices are very high. Stay half an hour away from the city, and you will pay far less for a much larger room. So the hotels which really aim to please, despite their popularity, are the ones which get our highest praise.

Introduction

- Murano glass chandeliers (hideous ones)
- Venetian marble floors (when coldly bare)
- Silk damask furnishing fabric (when overdone)
- 'Continental' breakfasts with inedible cardboard bread
- Hideous minibars
- Inadequate storage space
- Endless white-tiled bathrooms
- Too many bathrooms with shower only, no bathtub

Readers' reports

To all the hundreds of readers who have written with comments on hotels, a sincere 'thank-you'. We attach great importance to your comments and absorb them into the text each year. Please keep writing: for further information see page 32.

How to find an entry

In this guide, the whole-page entries, beginning on page 33, come first, followed by the half-page entries, which begin on page 134.

Hotels in Venice are featured first, subdivided into the city's *sestieri* or districts: San Marco, San Polo, Santa Croce, Castello, Dorsoduro, Cannaregio and the Lagoon Islands, including the Lido. In each subsection of Venice, entries are arranged in alphabetical order by name of hotel.

Hotels outside Venice are grouped according to the province in which they lie: first Veneto (which is the province in which Venice lies), then Lombardia (which accounts for the hotels on the western shores of Lake Garda – we do not explore this province any further as it does not lie in North-East Italy), followed by Friuli-Venezia Giulia, and Trentino-Alto Adige.

Within each of these regional sections, the entries are arranged in alphabetical order by nearest town. If several occur in one town, they are arranged in alphabetical order by name of hotel.

The half-page entries follow the same pattern: Venice, subdivided into its *sestieri*, followed by Veneto, Lombardia, Friuli-Venezia Giulia and Trentino-Alto Adige.

To find a hotel in a particular area, use the maps following this introduction to locate the appropriate pages.

To locate a specific hotel, whose name you know, or a hotel in a place you know, use the indexes at the back, which list entries both by name and by nearest place name.

How to read an entry

At the top of each entry is a coloured bar highlighting the name of the town or village, or in the case of Venice, district, where the establishment is located, along with a categorization which gives some clue to its character. These categories are, as far as possible, self-explanatory.

Fact boxes

The fact box given for each hotel follows a standard pattern; the explanation that follows is for full- and half-page entries.

Tel and Fax Numbers are the same whether you are calling from within a region or from another part of Italy. If you are calling from abroad, prefix the full number with the international code (39), and dial the initial zero of the area code.

E-mail and Website addresses were correct at the time of going to press but be aware that hotels sometimes change their server, and hotels which were not on-line may well be by now.

Location The location and setting of the hotel are briefly described; car parking facilities follow, except in Venice. In cities such as Padua and Verona, few hotels have their own car parking – most depend on arrangements with nearby garages. The prices are set by the garages and not by the hotels, so please check first.

In Venice hotels, under **vaporetto**, we tell you where the nearest *vaporetto* or water-bus landing stage is; we also indicate if the hotel has a water door on to a canal, so that you can arrive by gondola or water taxi. For those arriving by foot from the nearest *vaporetto* stop, lugging the luggage through the narrow streets and over the numerous little bridges that span the canals can be exhausting, especially if the hotel is none too close. If you prefer, you can enlist a porter to transport your bags, although they are very expensive. Porters are often available at San Marco and Rialto, but if you are arriving at any other landing stage, it is best to call your hotel and arrange for a porter to meet you.

Meals Under this heading we list the meals available. For breakfast, you may find either a continental breakfast or a self-service buffet breakfast (increasingly common) or both. We do not state whether a hotel provides room service, as this can vary from the provision of a cup of tea to full meals and 24-hour service. Generally, only the luxury hotels provide full room service, while small, smart ones might provide a limited service, and humble ones none at all; if in doubt, check with the hotel.

Prices The price bands given in this book refer to the cost of a standard double room in high season. The vast majority of hotels in this guide have both low and high season rates; many have a mid-season rate in between. It's often difficult to know when is low and when is high season (Carnival time in February is classed as high season) and in practice some hoteliers will charge according to how full their hotel is when you want to stay. A wide discrepancy between rooms is usually reflected in their prices; a small single room can be a fraction of the price of a suite in the same hotel.

The price band given reflects the cost of breakfast. This generally refers to a continental breakfast, although it may be buffet style. Many hotels will include a continental or light buffet breakfast in the price and offer other dishes at extra cost.

In many of the more remote country hotels, half-board is obligatory, especially out of season. Where this is the case, we have indicated it.

Check the price first. To avoid unpleasant surprises, always double-check the price at the time of booking. Sometimes prices go up after we have been to press, sometimes there are seasonal or other variations.

L	under L250,000
LL	L250,000-L400,000
LLL	L400,000-L600,000
LLLL	over L600,000

Rooms Under this heading we indicate the number and type – single, double, triple, family and suites – and whether the rooms have baths (usually with shower or shower attachment as well) or just showers. Unless stated you can assume that the bath or shower room will include a WC and washbasin. If you particularly want a bathtub (*bagno*) in your bathroom rather than just a shower, you should make this clear when you book, in case the receptionist thinks you simply mean you want a room with a bathroom.

If you have a large number of people to accommodate, do ask the hotel if rooms can be arranged to suit you. Although hotels may have one or two suites, rooms are generally not large, but sometimes connecting rooms are available. Very often the hotel will be able to supply a third bed in a double or twin room for a supplement.

Of the facilities we list in the rooms, in most cases the telephones will be direct-dial. In the most recently renovated hotels you may also find a fax/modem point. Many hotels now have cable or satellite TV in addition to the normal terrestrial channels: check with the hotel as to which, if any, foreign channels are available. We have not listed central heating as a facility, as all the hotels in the book have this; we do, however, indicate when a hotel has air-conditioning. Most hotels in the guide do, although in a few cases, this may mean bulky free-standing units.

Facilities Under facilities we list: public rooms; lift; courtyard, garden or terrace; indoor or outdoor swimming pool; tennis court; fitness and sauna facilities.

Credit cards We use the following abbreviations:
    AE   American Express

DC	Diners Club
MC	MasterCard (Access/Eurocard)
V	Visa (Barclaycard/Bank Americard/Carte Bleue etc)

Children Children are generally welcome in Italian hotels (and restaurants), so much so that in this guide we have not included this category in our fact box. Many hotels offer discounts on third beds for children sharing their parents' room.

Disabled Venice hotels are not the most suitable for those in wheelchairs, and many of the hotels in this guide are without lifts or special facilities. Where facilities exist, they are indicated.

Pets 'Accepted' means that the hotel is happy to accommodate well-behaved small animals. Sometimes they stipulate that animals are not allowed in public rooms. A small daily fee may be charged.

Closed Venice hotels rarely close. A handful shut down for a short period in winter. The same goes for hotels on the Veneto Plain. Hotels around Lake Garda, however, and in the mountains, are much more prone to periods of closure. Dates vary considerably, but as a rule, Lake Garda hotels close during the winter, while mountain hotels are open for the skiing season and high summer, but may close for a period in spring or early summer and again in autumn/early winter. The dates we give under the heading 'Closed' are those supplied to us by the hotel.

The final entry in a fact box is the name of the **Proprietor**(s). Where a hotel is run by a manager, we give his or her name.

Hotel location maps

North-Eastern Italy

Venice and its Lagoon

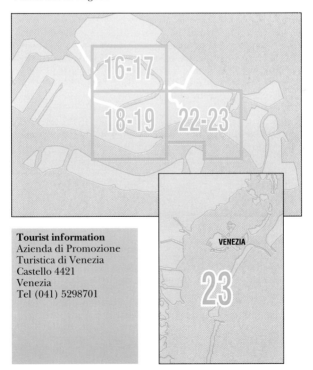

Tourist information
Azienda di Promozione
Turistica di Venezia
Castello 4421
Venezia
Tel (041) 5298701

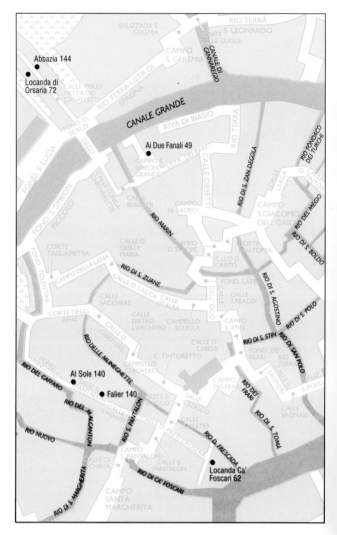

Cannaregio
Very much a residential area, full of charm and character, Cannaregio is bounded to the north by the Lagoon (Fondamente Nuove is the main starting point for *vaporetti* to the islands), and to the south by a long sweep of the Grand Canal. Most prized of the many lovely *palazzi* along here is the Ca' d'Oro, with its pink, sugar-spun Venetian Gothic façade. The bulk of tourists are drawn to Lista di Spagna and Strada Nova, two sections of the route from the station to the Rialto, leaving the rest of the district delightfully quiet at all times of the year. Don't miss the Ghetto, the world's oldest, nor the wonderfully over-the-top interior of Gesuiti, near Fondamente Nuove.

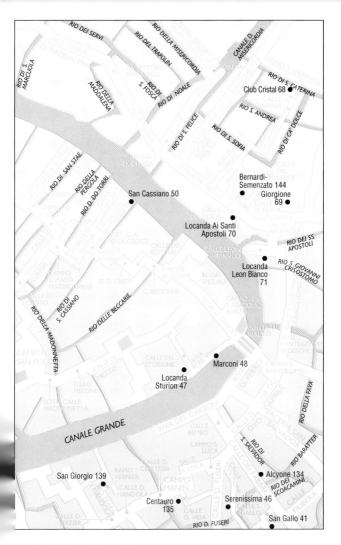

San Polo and Santa Croce

The *sestiere* of San Polo is lively and full of little shops, restaurants and bars, and of course, the colourful Rialto markets. Trading began here in the 11thC, and ever since, the *erberia* and *pescheria* markets have flourished. For just as long, the Rialto Bridge has attracted people; today it swarms with tourists, and the canal below is equally thick with river traffic. Built in 1588, it marks the centre of the city. Also in San Polo is the great Frari church, and Tintoretto's remarkable cycle of paintings in the Scuola di San Rocco. Santa Croce is mainly a humble area, with the vast car park, Piazzale Roma, as well as a stretch of *palazzi* along the Grand Canal, including one of our hotels.

17

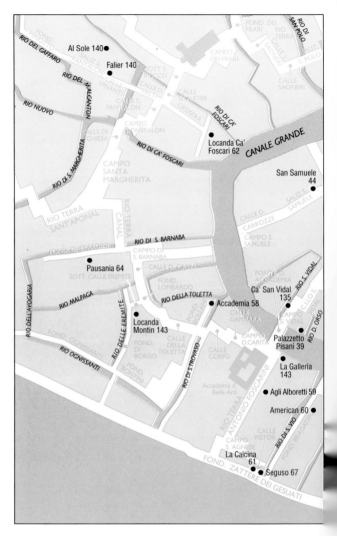

Dorsoduro

Only in 1854 was a second bridge constructed to cross the Grand Canal; in 1932 it was replaced with a temporary wooden structure, but, much loved, it has remained in place to this day as the Accademia Bridge which links the *sestieri* of San Marco and Dorsoduro. Bordered on one side by the Grand Canal, on the other by the wide Giudecca Canal, and criss-crossed by tributaries, Dorsoduro is tranquil and picturesque, yet close to the main sights. Its chief attractions are the Accademia Gallery and the Peggy Guggenheim Collection, as well as the churches of Santa Maria della Salute and Gesuati. Dig deeper and you will find the lovely and very old church of San Nicolò dei Mendicoli,

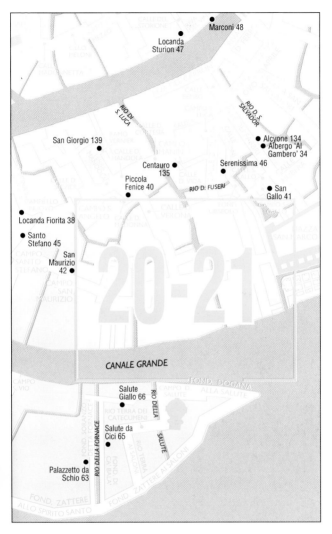

the gondola boatyard, and charming little spaces such as Campiello Barbaro and Campo San Barnaba. One of the greatest pleasures of Dorsoduro is to linger at a pavement café along the sun-soaked Zattere.

San Marco

Piazza San Marco is the heart of Venice, a fitting space from which to admire the great Basilica and Doge's Palace. Napoleon called it the 'most elegant drawing room in Europe' and on a balmy summer's night when the café orchestras are playing and the swirling daytime crowds have dwindled, his description is still apt. On one side of the Piazza is the Lagoon; on the other, ▶

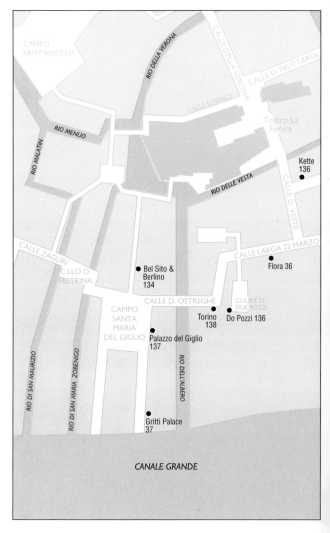

narrow streets full of shops, both for tourists and locals, fan out over the network of canals. In this district you will also find the opera house, Teatro La Fenice – or what's left of it – the spacious Campo Santo Stefano and the charming Bovolo staircase, tucked away in a quiet corner. You will also find the greatest concentration of charming small hotels.

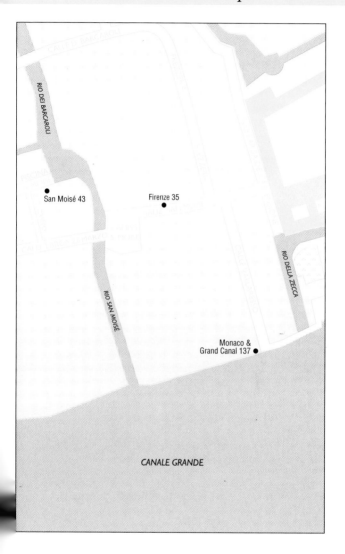

Hotel location maps

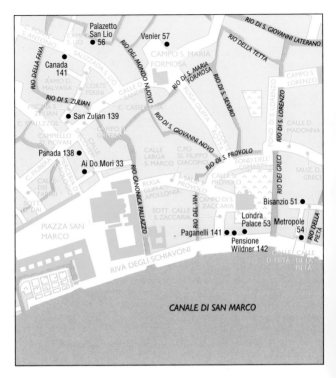

Castello

A marvellously varied district, Castello includes the mighty Riva degli Schiavoni, whose many hotels enjoy unrivalled views across the Lagoon to the island of San Giorgio Maggiore, with its landmark church of the same name by Palladio. Behind the waterfront lies a different Venice: quiet, dusty squares, pretty canals and lovely paintings – principally in San Giovanni in Bragora, Santa Maria Formosa, San Zaccaria, Scuola di San Giorgio degli Schiavoni, Fondazione Querini Stampalia and Santi Giovanni e Paolo. To the west is Arsenale, from where sprang the city's great maritime prowess.

Venetian Lagoon Islands

No visit to Venice is complete without a trip to at least some of the islands in the magical, mysterious Lagoon. Many centuries ago the people of the mainland were forced by invaders to seek refuge amongst the sandbanks; they built protective walls and thriving communities grew up, now long since disappeared. Murano has been a centre of glass-blowing since medieval times; San Michele is the cemetery island, and includes the tombs of famous artists and writers; Burano is packed with gaily painted houses; Torcello is the enigmatic cradle of the Venetian civilization, with only two beautiful churches to remind us of its days of supremacy; the Lido, developed in the 19thC is both city suburb and seaside resort, and retains the faintly melancholy air of the once-fashionable. Its great hotels are filled with conventions, but

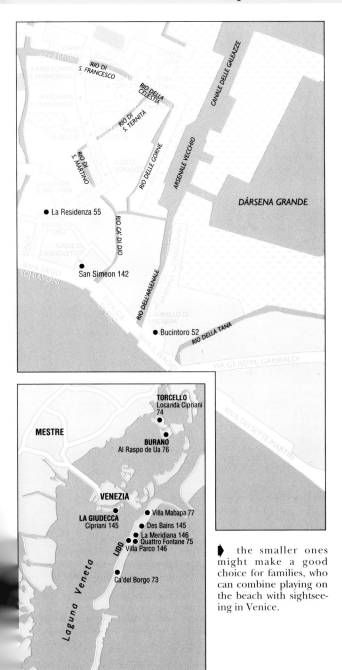

RIO DI
S. FRANCESCO

RIO DELLA
CELESTIA

CANALE DELLE GALEAZZE

RIO DI
S. TERNITÀ

RIO DELLE GORNE

ARSENALE VECCHIO

RIO DI
S. MARTINO

CORTE
SORANZA

DÁRSENA GRANDE

● La Residenza 55

RIO CA' DI DIO

CALLE D.
CAGNOLETTO

RIVA DEGLI
SCHIAVONI

● San Simeon 142

RIO DELL'ARSENALE

CAMPIELLO D.
MALVASIA

● Bucintoro 52

RIO DELLA TANA

VIA GIUSEPPE GARIBALDI

RIVA DEI SETTE MARTIRI

TORCELLO
Locanda Cipriani
74

MESTRE

BURANO
Al Raspo de Ua 76

VENEZIA

LA GIUDECCA
Cipriani 145

● Villa Mabapa 77

● Des Bains 145

● La Meridiana 146

LIDO

● Quattro Fontane 75
● Villa Parco 146

● Ca'del Borgo 73

Laguna Veneta

 the smaller ones
might make a good
choice for families, who
can combine playing on
the beach with sightsee-
ing in Venice.

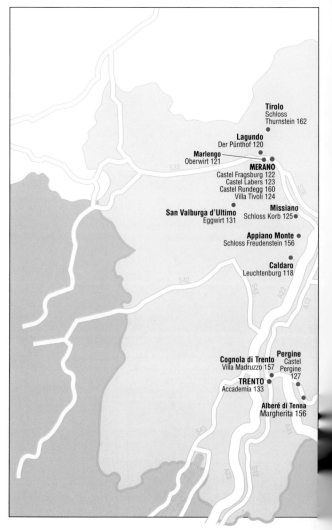

Tirolo
Schloss
Thurnstein 162

Lagundo
Der Pünthof 120

Marlengo
Oberwirt 121

MERANO
Castel Fragsburg 122
Castel Labers 123
Castel Rundegg 160
Villa Tivoli 124

San Valburga d'Ultimo
Eggwirt 131

Missiano
Schloss Korb 125

Appiano Monte
Schloss Freudenstein 156

Caldaro
Leuchtenburg 118

Cognola di Trento
Villa Madruzzo 157

Pergine
Castel
Pergine
127

TRENTO
Accademia 133

Alberé di Tenna
Margherita 156

Trentino-Alto Adige
The province of Trentino-Alto Adige is a world away from Venice and its great plain. It feels like Austria, has a special autonomous statute and is largely German-speaking. Owners and staff of the Alpine hotels you will find in its mountains may not even speak Italian ... you are more likely to be greeted in German, and they may speak English. Place names are extremely confusing, as each town and village, mountain and valley has both an Italian and German name. We have given the Italian translation, occasionally referring to the German as well. Hotels are often Tyrolean chalets, with wooden furniture, ceramic stoves, traditional fabrics; the food too, is mainly Austrian: dumplings,

Hotel location maps

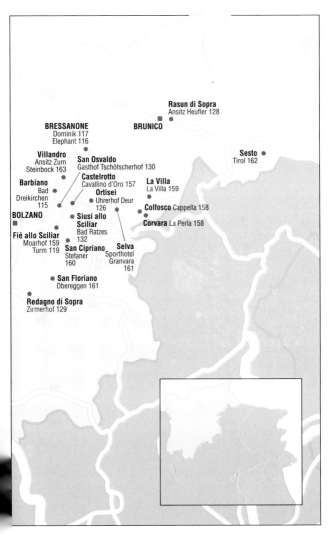

Rasun di Sopra Ansitz Heufler 128

BRESSANONE Dominik 117 Elephant 116

BRUNICO

Villandro Ansitz Zum Steinbock 163

San Osvaldo Gasthof Tschötscherhof 130

Sesto Tirol 162

Barbiano Bad Dreikirchen 115

Castelrotto Cavallino d'Oro 157

La Villa La Villa 159

Ortisei *Uhrerhof Deur* 126

Colfosco Cappella 158

BOLZANO

Siusi allo Sciliar Bad Ratzes 132

Corvara La Perla 158

Fié allo Sciliar Moarhof 159 Turm 119

San Cipriano Stefaner 160

Selva Sporthotel Granvara 161

San Floriano Obereggen 161

Redagno di Sopra Zirmhof 129

goulash and *sauerkraut* feature on the simpler menus, while the more sophisticated hotels serve creative variations on the theme. The scenery amongst the Dolomites is breathtakingly beautiful, and there are plenty of activities to pursue both in winter and summer.

Tourist information

Piazza Walther 8	132 Corso 111	9 Viale Stazione
Bolzano 39100	Novembre	Bressanone
Trentino-Alto Adige	Trento	Tel (0472) 836401
Tel (0471) 970660	Tel (0461) 980000	

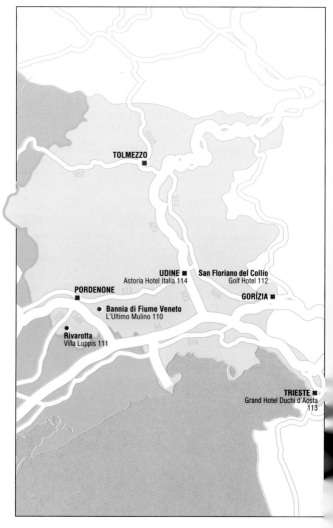

TOLMEZZO ■

UDINE ■
Astoria Hotel Italia 114

San Floriano del Collio
Golf Hotel 112

PORDENONE ■

GORÍZIA ■

● Bannia di Fiume Veneto
L'Ultimo Mulino 110

● Rivarotta
Villa Luppis 111

TRIESTE ■
Grand Hotel Duchi d'Aosta
113

26

Friuli-Venezia Giulia

The province accounts for the eastern part of the Veneto Plain as it curves towards the border with Slovenia. To the north and the border with Austria it rises to the Carnic Alps with its alpine meadows and pine forests. Some 20 years ago the area was devastated by an earthquake. Some of the most beautiful and verdant scenery in all Italy can be found in this corner of the country, and yet it is hardly visited, and hotels are thin on the ground. There are some old-fashioned hostelries in Tolmezzo and the beautifully situated spa town of Arta Terme. The main cities are Trieste, with its air of faded grandeur, and Udine, a busy industrial town with a lovely old *piazza* and cathedral. Our small selection of hotels can be found mainly in the west of the province.

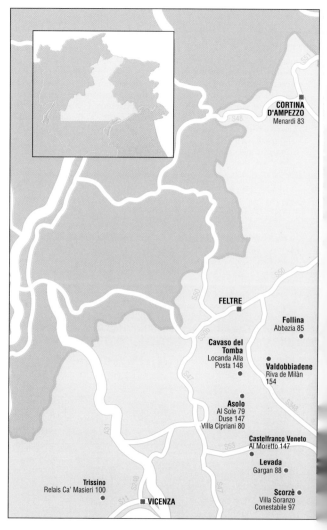

CORTINA D'AMPEZZO
Menardi 83

FELTRE

Follina
Abbazia 85

Cavaso del Tomba
Locanda Alla
Posta 148

Valdobbiadene
Riva de Milàn
154

Asolo
Al Sole 79
Duse 147
Villa Cipriani 80

Castelfranco Veneto
Al Moretto 147

Levada
Gargan 88

Trissino
Relais Ca' Masieri 100

Scorzè
Villa Soranzo
Conestabile 97

VICENZA

North Veneto
The province of Veneto accounts for much of the great Veneto
Plain, but to its north it thrusts through the mountains to reach
the Austrian border. The bulk of our hotels are on the plain, in
both countryside and in the plain's great cities, Vicenza, Padua
and Treviso. If you want to stay within easy reach of Venice, there
are plenty of choices. To the north of the province, where the
foothills of the Dolomites begin to rise from the flat landscape,
you will find some delightful places; the charming hilltop village
of Asolo is particularly well served. To the west, there are choices
in the vibrant and lovely city of Verona, in the fertile wine-coun-
try around it, and along the eastern shores of Lake Garda.

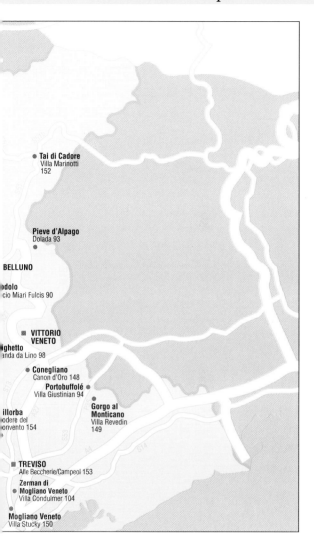

Tai di Cadore
Villa Marinotti
152

Pieve d'Alpago
Dolada 93

BELLUNO

dolo
cio Miari Fulcis 90

**VITTORIO
VENETO**

ghetto
anda da Lino 98

Conegliano
Canon d'Oro 148

Portobuffolé
Villa Giustinian 94

**Gorgo al
Monticano**
Villa Revedin
149

illorba
odere del
onvento 154

TREVISO
Alle Beccherie/Campeol 153

**Zerman di
Mogliano Veneto**
Villa Condulmer 104

Mogliano Veneto
Villa Stucky 150

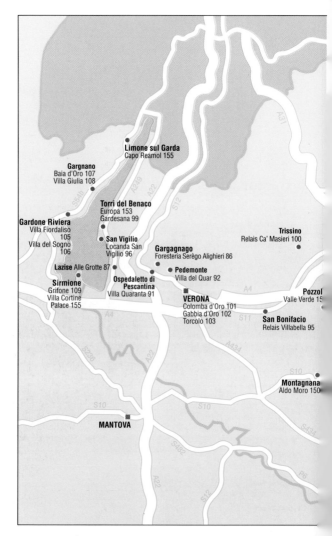

Limone sul Garda
Capo Reamol 155

Gargnano
Baia d'Oro 107
Villa Giulia 108

Torri del Benaco
Europa 153
Gardesana 99

Gardone Riviera
Villa Fiordaliso 105
Villa del Sogno 106

San Vigilio
Locanda San Vigilio 96

Gargagnago
Foresteria Serègo Alighieri 86

Trissino
Relais Ca' Masieri 100

Lazise Alle Grotte 87

Ospedaletto di Pescantina
Villa Quaranta 91

Pedemonte
Villa del Quar 92

Sirmione
Grifone 109
Villa Cortine Palace 155

VERONA
Colomba d'Oro 101
Gabbia d'Oro 102
Torcolo 103

Pozzol
Valle Verde 15

San Bonifacio
Relais Villabella 95

Montagnana
Aldo Moro 150

MANTOVA

Lombardia and some Veneto

The only part of the province of Lombardia that concerns this guide is the area on the western shores of Lake Garda, the largest lake in Italy. It makes an ideal summertime playground, where you can windsurf, sail or cruise the lake by ferry. With a backdrop of snow-capped mountains, the shores are strung along with pretty villages, little harbours and waterfront promenades. To the south, the Sirmione Peninsula points into the lake, and the old town of Sirmione is the most picturesque of all.

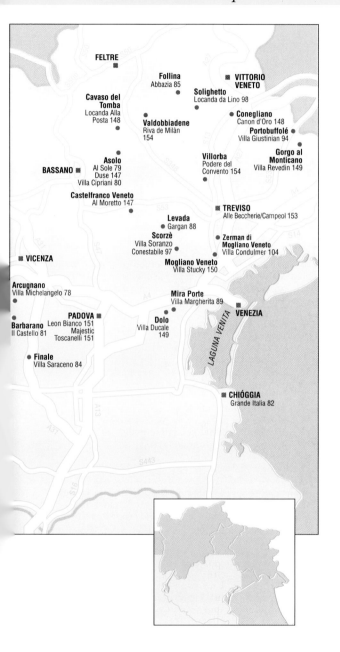

FELTRE

Follina
Abbazia 85

VITTORIO VENETO

Cavaso del Tomba
Locanda Alla Posta 148

Solighetto
Locanda da Lino 98

Valdobbiadene
Riva de Milàn 154

Conegliano
Canon d'Oro 148

Portobuffolé
Villa Giustinian 94

Gorgo al Monticano
Villa Revedin 149

Villorba
Podere del Convento 154

Asolo
Al Sole 79
Duse 147
Villa Cipriani 80

BASSANO

Castelfranco Veneto
Al Moretto 147

TREVISO
Alle Beccherie/Campeol 153

Levada
Gargan 88

Scorzè
Villa Soranzo Conestabile 97

Zerman di Mogliano Veneto
Villa Condulmer 104

VICENZA

Mogliano Veneto
Villa Stucky 150

Arcugnano
Villa Michelangelo 78

Mira Porte
Villa Margherita 89

VENEZIA

PADOVA
Leon Bianco 151
Majestic Toscanelli 151

Dolo
Villa Ducale 149

LAGUNA VENITA

Barbarano
Il Castello 81

Finale
Villa Saraceno 84

CHIÓGGIA
Grande Italia 82

31

Please write and tell us about your experiences of small hotels, guest houses and inns, whether good or bad, whether listed in this edition or not. As well as hotels in Venice & North-East Italy, we are interested in charming small hotels in: Britain, Ireland, the rest of Italy, France, Spain, Portugal, Germany, Switzerland and other European countries, as well as the east and west coasts of the United States.

The address to write to is:

> *Charming Small Hotel Guides,*
> Duncan Petersen Publishing Ltd,
> 31 Ceylon Road,
> London, W14 OPY
> England.

Checklist
Please use a separate sheet of paper for each report; include your name, address and telephone number on each sheet.
   Your reports are particularly welcome if they are typed and organized under the following headings:

> Name of establishment
> Town or village
> Full address and postcode
> Telephone number
> Time and duration of visit
> The building and setting
> Public rooms
> Bedrooms and bathrooms
> Standards of maintenance, housekeeping
> Standards of comfort and decoration
> Atmosphere, welcome and service
> Food
> Value for money

We assume that in writing you have no objection to your views being published unpaid, either verbatim or in an edited version. Names of major outside contributors are acknowledged in the guide, at the editor's discretion.

San Marco

Town guest-house

Ai Do Mori

We had great difficulty finding the Ai Do Mori – reception is on the first floor and only a lantern discreetly displays the name on the street. We arrived to find the vivacious young owner divulging tips to some guests: "Don't take a gondola on the Grand Canal. A *vaporetto* is much cheaper. Take a gondola on the little canals and see a different Venice."

At the time of our visit there were no facilities for serving breakfast and only half the bedrooms had bathrooms, but Antonella Bernardi is constantly making changes and plans to add a breakfast room and bathrooms shortly. We suspect that in a year or so it will be upgraded from its one-star status.

The modest white-walled bedrooms are spacious and light. Nos 6 and 7 have rustic beams, but by far the most desirable is the one Antonella endearingly calls "the painter room". Up a steep staircase, tucked under the eaves, it is small – just accommodating the double bed and a few carefully chosen pieces of furniture – but has a small suntrap of a roof terrace, from where you can almost reach out and touch the figures on the Basilica San Marco; and this for just L220,000 a night.

Nearby Piazza San Marco; San Zulian.

Calle Larga San Marco, San Marco 658, 30124 Venezia
Tel 041 5204817/5289293
Fax 041 5205328
Location near junction with Calle Spadaria, just N of Piazzetta dei Leoni; **vaporetto** San Marco
Meals none
Prices L
Rooms 11; 10 double and twin, triple and family, 4 with bath, 2 with shower, 4 with washbasin; 1 single with washbasin; all rooms have phone, TV, air-conditioning, hairdrier, safe
Credit cards MC, V
Disabled not suitable
Pets not accepted
Closed 3 weeks in Jan
Proprietor Antonella Bernardi

San Marco

Town guest-house

Albergo 'Al Gambero'

Sandro Rossi has transformed his simple guest-house, a one-time haven for students and backpackers, into a smart little hotel with pretty honey-coloured damask walls and striped curtains and small, but comfortable bedrooms, all done up in the same vein with attractive repro furniture, tiled floors and spanking new marble bathrooms. There are 13 old-style rooms with no bathrooms (though they do all have basins). Recently refurnished and, though still pretty basic, at 150,000L they offer excellent value for San Marco. Most of the bedrooms are off long corridors, up flights of marble stairs from the first-floor reception. There is no lift. The hotel is classified a one star and will continue to be until all the rooms have been renovated.

From the little apricot and green breakfast room beyond the reception, Signor Rossi assures us that in summer you can hear the *gondolieri* serenades. The focal point of this room is a gleaming copper and brass *espresso* machine. On the ground floor Le Bistrot de Venise serves Venetian and French dishes and offers hotel guests a 10 per cent discount. In fine weather meals can be eaten in a large, pleasant garden. New to the guide.

Nearby Piazza San Marco, San Zulian.

Calle dei Fabbri, San Marco 4687, 30124 Venezia
Tel 041 5224384/5201420
Fax 041 5200431
E-mail hotgamb@tin.it
Location in shopping street just north of Piazza San Marco; **vaporetto** San Marco, Rialto or water taxi
Meals breakfast
Prices L
Rooms 27 double and twin, 14 with bath; all rooms have phone; new rooms have TV, air-conditioning, minibar, hairdrier, safe
Facilities breakfast room
Credit cards MC, V
Disabled not suitable
Pets not accepted
Closed never
Proprietor Sandro Rossi

San Marco

Town hotel

Firenze

The distinguishing features of the Firenze are its rooftop terrace – reached from the top floor by an external staircase – where you can breakfast in summer whilst picking out the landmarks, and the three bedrooms with private terrace which cost no more than ones without.

The building, just along from the florid, blackened façade of San Moisè, has a fine marble-and-iron art nouveau front (in need of restoration – the owner has plans); at the turn of the century it was an Austrian hat factory, as the splendid first floor windows announce. Inside, a recent total renovation has left the bedrooms uniform: unadorned Venetian marble floors (not cosy), peach-coloured walls, pale green headboards and matching cupboards, pretty Murano glass wall lights and white ruched net curtains. The first-floor breakfast room was designed to echo the famous café Florian in Piazza San Marco, with polished wood benches and tables lining the walls, but it doesn't quite come off and feels merely awkward. Choose the Firenze – managed with good humour by its owner, Signor Fabris – during the summer when you can make use of the terrace.

Nearby Piazza San Marco.

Salizzada San Moisè, San Marco 1490, 30124 Venezia
Tel 041 5222858
Fax 041 5202668
E-mail hotelfirenze@flashnet.it
Website www.elmoro.com/firenze
Location 30 m from Piazza San Marco, alongside San Moisè; **vaporetto** San Marco
Meals breakfast
Prices LL
Rooms 25; 22 double, 3 single, all with bath; all rooms have phone, TV, air-conditioning, minibar, hairdrier, safe
Facilities breakfast room, rooftop terrace, lift
Credit cards AE, MC, V
Children accepted
Disabled not suitable
Pets accepted
Closed never
Proprietor Paolo Fabris

San Marco

Town hotel

Flora

Such is the popularity of this small hotel, tucked away down a cul-de-sac close to San Marco, that to get a room here you have to book weeks, even months in advance. You only need to glimpse the garden to know why it is sought after. Creepers, fountains and flowering shrubs cascading from stone urns create an enchanting setting for breakfast, tea or an evening drink in summer.

The lobby is small and inviting, enhanced by the views of the garden through a glass arch; the atmosphere is one of friendly efficiency. There are some charming double bedrooms with painted carved antiques and other typically Venetian furnishings, but beware of other comparatively spartan rooms, some of which are barely big enough for one, let alone two. Coveted rooms include two on the ground floor facing the garden and the three spacious corner rooms, the topmost of which has a marvellous view of Santa Maria della Salute. These rooms represent value for money; others do not. The venerable Flora has been run by the charming Romanelli family, father, son and grandson, for the past 38 years.

Nearby Piazza San Marco.

Calle Larga XXII Marzo, San Marco 2283/a, 30124 Venezia
Tel 041 5205844
Fax 041 5228217
E-mail info@hotelflora.it
Fax www.hotelflora.it
Location 300 m from Piazza San Marco in cul-de-sac off Calle Larga XXII Marzo; **vaporetto** San Marco
Meals breakfast
Prices LL
Rooms 44; 32 double and twin, 6 single, 6 family, all with bath

or shower; all rooms have phone, TV, air-conditioning, hairdrier, safe
Facilities reading room, breakfast room, bar, lift, garden
Credit cards AE, DC, MC, V
Disabled two rooms on ground floor
Pets accepted
Closed never
Proprietors Roger and Joel Romanelli

San Marco

Town hotel

Gritti Palace

Of the three great hotels in Venice – the Danieli, the Cipriani and the Gritti – this is our favourite, and the one which most closely reflects the spirit of this incomparably beautiful city. The Danieli is far too large for us to include, but at under 100 rooms apiece, we have allowed ourselves the liberty of including the other two: they are individual and intimate, and anyway no hotel guide to Venice would be complete without them.

All the bedrooms at the Gritti, the 15thC *palazzo* of Doge Andrea Gritti which opened as a hotel in 1948, are stunning; at least all the ones we saw were – tell us if you disagree. Of the eight exquisite Canal Views suites, our favourite was the Hemingway, in restful shades of pale green. Service is immaculate, the atmosphere patrician yet friendly, and the prices, whilst lofty, far more reasonable than the Cipriani's. And, as Somerset Maugham pointed out, there are few greater pleasures in life than taking a drink on the terrace at sunset, watching the Salute opposite bathed in lovely colour. Before bed, he advises, glance at the portrait of old Andrea Gritti, who, after a tumultuous life, lived his last years here in peace.

Nearby Teatro La Fenice; Piazza San Marco; Accademia.

Campo Santa Maria del Giglio, San Marco 2467, 30124 Venezia
Tel 041 794611
Fax 041 5200942
E-mail reso73_grittipalace@itt.sheraton.com
Website www.luxurycollection.com
Location in *campo* on Grand Canal; **vaporetto** Santa Maria del Giglio or by water taxi
Meals breakfast, lunch, dinner
Prices LLLL
Rooms 93; 80 double and twin, 7 single, 6 suites, all with bath; all rooms have phone, TV, fax/modem point, air-conditioning, minibar, hairdrier
Facilities sitting room, dining room, bar, meeting room, lift, terrace
Credit cards AE, DC, MC, V
Disabled no special facilities, but access possible
Pets accepted
Closed never
Manager Massimo Feriani

San Marco

Town guest-house

Locanda Fiorita

If you are looking for rock-bottom prices and a quiet yet central location, look no further than this bargain one star, a red-painted villa tucked away in a quiet, little-visited square off Campo Santo Stefano. Rooms are small and functional, with modern white furniture which include desks, bedside tables, even beds. Our reporter found her bed surprisingly comfortable, but noted the skimpy towels and lack of shelves, though there was plenty of cupboard space in her room. 'With its beamed ceiling, mint-coloured walls and large windows it was a perfectly pleasant room in which to wake up,' she comments, 'especially when one reflects on what it cost'. No. 10 is the 'honeymoon room', with cupids painted on the wall and a tiny, rather public terrace. Breakfast is taken either at wooden tables set along the wall in the reception area, or, more comfortably, in your room. In summer, the terrace which runs along the front of the building is covered in a pergola of vines, and there are colourful flowers in window boxes. An eight-room annexe has opened nearby, but it is not as pleasant (despite more facilities) and is more expensive than the main hotel.

Nearby Piazza San Marco; Accademia gallery.

Campiello Nuovo, Santo Stefano, San Marco 3457, 30124 Venezia
Tel 041 5234754
Fax 041 5228043
E-mail locafior@tin.it
Location a little square off Campo Santo Stefano/Calle dei Frati; **vaporetto** San Samuele
Meals breakfast
Prices L
Rooms 10; 8 double, 2 single, 9 with shower and WC, 1 without; all rooms have phone, fan, hair-drier; 5 have TV
Facilities reception/breakfast area, small terrace
Credit cards AE, MC, V
Disabled access difficult
Pets accepted
Closed never
Proprietor Renato Colombera

San Marco

Apartments in private house

Palazzetto Pisani

Since the 19thC the austere Palazzo Pisani has been the Conservatory of Music; you can often here music wafting from its windows. Behind it, reached by a tiny alley, is the unobstrusive entrance to Palazzetto Pisani, which stands on the Grand Canal. This is the ancestral home of the once-powerful Pisani family, now occupied by Contessa Maria Pia Ferre, direct descendent of Alvise Pisani, who became doge in 1735. It's a wonderful anachronism whose glorious faded grandeur transports one to another age. The vast main apartment, on the *piano nobile*, has just one bedroom – the doge's, a beautiful drawing room with balconies on the Grand Canal, a delightful sitting room full of family souvenirs, and two dining rooms (in the larger of which you can hold a cocktail party or a dinner for up to 80 people). A maid is on hand, and a cook, should you wish it. Downstairs is a small one-bedroom apartment with a remarkable original bathroom.

If you are rich enough, invite your friends to join you in Venice, settle yourselves in the Palazzetto Pisani, and throw a party for them. New to the guide.

Nearby Accademia gallery, Piazza San Marco.

Calle di Ca'Genova, San Marco 2814, 30124 Venezia
Tel 041 5232550
Fax 041 5232550
E-mail palpisani@tin.it
Location corner of Grand Canal and Rio dell'Orso, off Campo Santo Stefano; vaporetto Accademia or water taxi
Prices on application
Rooms ground-floor suite with one double bedroom, ante-room, kitchen, bathroom; first-floor apartment with one double bedroom, shower room, drawing room, sitting room, 2 dining/reception rooms, kitchen; maid service, cook available
Credit cards not accepted
Disabled not suitable
Pets on ground floor only
Closed never
Proprietor Contessa Maria Pia Ferre

San Marco

Town hotel

Piccola Fenice

The Teatro La Fenice has now begun to rise from the ashes, after the disatrous fire which rendered it a stark shell for several years. The famous adjacent hotel, Fenice et des Artistes, where performers used to put up, was looking too gloomy and faded for us to include, but we were impressed by its new sister hotel, the Piccola Fenice. This consists of seven suites sleeping between two and six people, all with large rooms, including bathrooms tiled in pretty colours, with generous basins, attractive furniture, and facilities for making breakfast. On the wide first-floor landing there is a huge Murano glass chandelier and a sitting area with desk and armchairs. The topmost apartment would be perfect for a family. There is a little children's room, with two beds covered in fresh white bedspreads, and a beamed master bedroom with elegant bed and en suite bathroom, plus a kitchenette with microwave, a circular dining table, a double sofa bed and an enchanting little wooden-railed terrace with views across the rooftops to Salute. Two people could really spread out in here, and would pay only L360,000 for a night – in terms of space, a real bargain.

Nearby Bovolo Staircase; Piazza San Marco.

Calle della Madonna, San Marco 3614, 30124 Venezia
Tel 041 5204909
Fax 041 5204909
Location off Campo Sant' Angelo, near Teatro La Fenice; **vaporetto** Sant'Angelo
Meals breakfast (at adjacent Hotel Fenice et des Artistes)
Prices LL; weekly rates available
Rooms 7 suites sleeping 2–6, all with bath; all rooms have phone, TV, air-conditioning, hairdrier, safe; 6 rooms have fridge, tea/coffee making facilities
Facilities sitting area, stairlift
Credit cards AE, DC, MC, V
Disabled stairlift for wheelchairs to first-floor rooms
Pets not accepted
Closed Jan
Proprietor Michele Facchini

San Marco

Town hotel

San Gallo

All you see from the outside is a rather dilapidated cinema, but don't be put off, the entrance to the San Gallo is up a flight of stone steps and through a heavy internal door. Buzz the buzzer and you will be admitted to a room that is a breath of fresh air with not a patch of silk damask in sight. This one large room fulfils the functions of reception, sitting and breakfast areas. Although the low ceiling bristles with unstained 14thC beams, it manages to be light and airy, and is freshly decorated in white with panels of mellow *faux* marble. Smart striped sofas and chairs cluster around wooden tables, and a little bar is tucked into one corner.

Luca Folin, the energetic and committed owner/manager who originally renovated the San Gallo, sold the hotel two years ago to Franco Ferigo, whose plans include redecorating the bedrooms. They are currently done up simply, with somewhat traditional furnishings – velvet button bedheads, Murano chandeliers, busy patterned floor tiles – not so much to our taste. But there is a glorious roof terrace where in summer you can breakfast amidst the potted plants.

Nearby Piazza San Marco; San Zulian.

Campo San Gallo, San Marco
1093/a, 30124 Venezia
Tel 041 5227311/5289877
Fax 041 5225702
E-mail sangallo@hotelsangallo.com
Website www.hotelsangallo.com
Location N of Piazza San Marco, E of Orseolo canal;
vaporetto San Marco
Meals breakfast
Prices LL
Rooms 12; 8 double and twin, 2 with bath, 6 with shower; 1 single, 3 triple or family, all with

shower; all rooms have phone, TV, air-conditioning, minibar, hairdrier
Facilities bar/breakfast/sitting room, roof terrace
Credit cards MC, V
Disabled not suitable
Pets accepted
Closed never
Proprietor Franco Ferigo

San Marco

San Maurizio

A very simple, inexpensive little hotel in a central location, with a certain something about it which lifts it out of the rut.

A pretty wrought-iron sign spotted just off Campo San Maurizio, along the route between Campo Santo Stefano and San Marco, first alerted us to the hotel whose entrance is reached down a tiny flowery passage. In the spacious lobby/breakfast room, white wrought-iron tables and chairs with red cushions, white walls and white-painted beams on the ceiling lend a delicate, summery air, and the reception desk – two stone lions supporting a stone slab – is an eye-catching feature that also adds a touch of class.

When we visited, bedrooms were in the process of being redecorated one by one, and the best, though plain, had character. No 4, for example, is charming and spacious, with two long windows on to a little terrace. A small first-floor landing had been thoughtfully decorated with table and chairs and Chinese vases. It remains to be seen how the hotel develops under new management. New to the guide: readers' reports would be particularly welcome.

Nearby Piazza San Marco; Accademia gallery; Rialto.

Campo San Maurizio, San Marco 2624, 30124 Venezia
Tel 041 5289712
Fax 041 5289712
Location just off Campo San Maurizio between Campo Santo Stefano and Piazza San Marco; vaporetto Santa Maria del Giglio
Meals breakfast
Prices LL
Rooms 11, 5 with shower, 6 sharing bathrooms; all rooms have phone, TV, air-condition-ing, minibar, safe, hairdrier
Facilities breakfast room, bar
Credit cards AE, DC, MC,V
Disabled not suitable
Pets accepted
Closed never
Proprietor Antonio Ghersani

San Marco

Town hotel

San Moisè

The interior is very Venetian, and not to everyone's taste; to us the lurid pink silk damask wallcoverings in the public rooms were more than a touch reminiscent of a high-class brothel, and the accompanying Murano glass chandeliers and wall lights appropriately garish examples of the genre. This is a matter of preference, however – some may find the decoration as elegant as it is evidently intended to be.

There are a handful of special rooms at the San Moisè – under the same ownership, and in the same mould as the Marconi (see page 44) and the San Cassiano (see page 46) – which are well worth seeking out. One has splendid carved mahogany furnishings and steps up to a little bathroom. Two others (Nos 8 and 22) have views straight down the Rio dei Barcaroli, a jolly and picturesque canal which is packed with gondolas and their camera-clicking cargo. Decorated in the same old-fashioned Venetian style as its sister hotels, the San Moisè struck us as being the best turned-out of the three with the friendliest staff. Its position, very central, yet tucked away at the end of a little street and on a canal, is enviable.

Nearby San Moisè; Teatro La Fenice; Piazza San Marco.

Piscina San Moisè, San Marco 2058, 30124 Venezia
Tel 041 5203755
Fax 041 5210670
E-mail sanmoise@sanmoise.it
Website www.sanmoise.it
Location off Calle Larga XXII Marzo, 2 mins walk from Piazza San Marco; **vaporetto** San Marco or water taxi
Meals breakfast
Prices LLL
Rooms 16; 13 double, twin and triple, 4 with bath, 9 with shower; 3 single, all with shower; all rooms have phone, TV, air-conditioning, minibar, hairdrier, safe
Facilities breakfast room
Credit cards AE, DC, MC, V
Disabled not suitable
Pets accepted
Closed never
Proprietor Franco Maschietto

San Marco

Town guest-house

San Samuele

A budget establishment with new young managers, a fresh lick of paint, 300-year old Venetian marble floors and a pleasant, airy feel to the bedrooms.

The *pensione* is installed on the upper floors of a pretty house in a wide street leading to the San Samuele vaporetto and traghetto landing stage. Ring the bell for admission, enter a pleasant little enclosed courtyard and start climbing the stairs, of which there are quite a few – this is a hotel for the young and fit.

All the bedrooms have been recently redecorated, their main decorative feature being a square of pink colour on the wall behind each low, skimpy-looking bed (an inspector informs us that they are adequately comfortable). Bathrooms are new, each enlivened by a jolly shower curtain. What gives these rooms the edge over others in the same price range, however, is the presence of not one but two large windows with views over the street. The two rooms at the back make up in quiet what they lack in light. Breakfast is served in the rooms. It's new to the guide, and, as we went to press, seems to be that rare phenomenon, a 'new discovery' – not yet written about in other guide books.

Nearby Accademia gallery; Frari; Campo Santo Stefano.

Salizzada San Samuele, San Marco 3358, 30124 Venezia
Tel 041 5205165
Fax 041 5205165
Location in quiet area of San Marco, between Campo Santo Stefano and Grand Canal; vaporetto San Samuele
Meals breakfast
Prices L
Rooms 10; 8 double, 2 single, 7 with shower; all rooms have phone
Credit cards not accepted

Disabled not suitable
Pets not accepted
Closed never
Proprietor San Samuele Association

San Marco

Santo Stefano

If you follow the popular route from Piazza San Marco to the Accademia gallery you will walk across the Campo Santo Stefano, a large, lively and rambling square whose church has an alarmingly tilted *campanile*.

Close to all the activity stands the Santo Stefano, a welcoming and well cared for little hotel whose front rooms have views of the square (although these are prone to noise). The hotel has long been a stalwart of our all-Italy guide, and on our latest visit we found that it had been acquired by an ambitious new owner, that prices had gone up, and that the little reception area and tiny breakfast room had been given a refreshing facelift: contemporary furniture, prettily painted ceiling beams and pillars, and marble wall panels to match the floor. Bedrooms, however, remain unchanged, and look dated and rather tired by comparison, though they have brand-new all-marble bathrooms and redecoration is planned. Some are very compact, but No. 11, with views across the *campo*, is light and spacious. There is a tiny courtyard terrace at the back of the hotel as well as one in front, where you can sip a coffee and watch the world go by.

Nearby Accademia gallery; Piazza San Marco.

Campo Santo Stefano, San Marco 2957, 30124 Venezia
Tel 041 5200166
Fax 041 5224460
Location on large square about 500 m W of Piazza San Marco; **vaporetto** San Samuele
Meals breakfast
Prices LLL
Rooms 11; 6 double and twin, 2 single, 3 triple or quadruple, all with shower; all rooms have phone, TV, air-conditioning, minibar, hairdrier, safe

Facilities breakfast room, courtyard, lift, front terrace
Credit cards MC, V
Disabled access difficult
Pets accepted
Closed never
Proprietor Roberto Quatrini

San Marco

Town guest-house

Serenissima

Readers' reports confirm that this is one of the most endearing and best-kept two-star hotels in town. Our inspector told us that she found it much pleasanter to stay here than in many a more expensive three star, and given its central location just a few paces from the Doge's Palace, Basilica and Piazza San Marco, she deemed it value for money – a rare experience in Venice. Bedrooms are admittedly on the small side (a triple will give two people more room), but neat and pretty, some with purpose-made wooden fittings, others – the ones that have been most recently redecorated – with more attractive Venetian painted headboards, cupboards and bedside tables. The neat, tiled bathrooms have proper shower enclosures, not curtains. Try for a room with a view on to the sunny little square at the back, empty but for its central well and very peaceful. Both the charming first-floor breakfast room and white-walled corridors are hung with attractive and colourful modern paintings – these alone seem to lift the Serenissima from the rut. Downstairs in reception there is a little bar. The hotel has been looked after with great care by the same family since 1960.

Nearby Piazza San Marco; Rialto; Bovolo staircase.

Calle Goldoni, San Marco 4486, 30124 Venezia
Tel 041 5200011
Fax 041 5223292
Location between Piazza San Marco and Rialto, close to Calle dei Fabbri; **vaporetto** San Marco, Rialto
Meals breakfast
Prices LL
Rooms 37; 29 double, twin and triple, 5 with bath, 24 with shower; 8 single, 2 with bath, 6 with shower; all rooms have phone, TV, air-conditioning, hairdrier
Facilities sitting area, breakfast room, bar
Credit cards AE, DC, MC, V
Disabled not suitable
Pets accepted
Closed after Carnival to mid-Mar
Proprietor Roberto dal Borgo

San Polo

Locanda Sturion

First you have to conquer the stairs, a seemingly endless flight which rises like a ladder from the ground floor to the hotel on the third floor. The friendly receptionist must be used to her guests collapsing in front of her desk, for she refrained from smirking when this inspector presented herself gulping for air. There is no porter, but receptionists will help with luggage.

Once you have recovered sufficiently to take in your surroundings, you will find them plush. Deep red silk fabric adorns the walls in several of the bedrooms (these are non-smoking), with pale silk damask in others. Furniture throughout is walnut and mahogany, with floors of Venetian marble or covered in deep red carpet. Two rooms look on to the Grand Canal. They are spacious for two people, and can sleep two extra, one on a bed cleverly hidden during the day in a wooden box masquerading as a cupboard. A little library of guidebooks, many in English, adds a homely touch.

Locanda Sturion, found in a dark street hung with washing, has long been a hostelry. It stands on the site of a 13thC house built for foreign merchants taking their wares to the market.
Nearby Rialto; Rialto markets; Ca' d'Oro.

Calle del Storione, San Polo 679, 30125 Venezia
Tel 041 5236243
Fax 041 5228378
E-mail sturion@tin.it
Website www.sayville.com/locanda-sturion.html
Location off Riva del Vin, close to Rialto Bridge **vaporetto** Rialto, San Silvestro
Meals breakfast
Prices LL
Rooms 11; 8 double, twin and triple, 3 family, 10 with bath, one with shower; all rooms have phone, TV, air-conditioning, minibar, hairdrier, safe
Facilities breakfast room
Credit cards AE, MC, V
Disabled not suitable
Pets accepted
Closed never
Proprietor Signor Fragiacomo

San Polo

Marconi

The Marconi is a typical Venice hotel, encapsulating both what is right and what is wrong about many of them. As so often, the location is enviable (although since it is right by Rialto Bridge, overlooking a stretch of Grand Canal thick with gondolas, it appeals to those wanting action rather than peace and quiet). The building is a 16thC *palazzo* with a 19thC entrance hall which has a glass and wood frontage, marbled pillars, velvet hangings and green and gold embossed ceiling. Best of all, the two rooms with balconies which overlook the Grand Canal cost no more than the rest, so you should try hard for one of them. Bedrooms are fairly simple, but mahogany furniture, carved bedheads and damask curtains lend an old-fashioned, grandiose air. There is double glazing throughout. Yet though the hotel was renovated only a few years ago, its dark wood fittings and rather dated fabrics give it a gloomy and rather musty air. And one senses that the staff, knowing that it is easy to fill the hotel, are not as interested in their guests' well-being as they might be. In other words, a hotel which lacks a heart and coasts along rather than strives. More reports please.

Nearby Rialto; Rialto markets; Ca' d'Oro.

Riva del Vin, San Polo 729, 30125 Venezia
Tel 041 5222068
Fax 041 5229700
E-mail marconi@marconi.it
Website www.marconi.it
Location beside Rialto Bridge, opposite the *vaporetto* landing stage **vaporetto** Rialto
Meals breakfast
Prices LLL
Rooms 28; 23 double or triple, 3 single, 2 family, all with bath or shower; all rooms have phone, TV, air-conditioning, hairdrier, safe
Facilities breakfast room, terrace
Credit cards AE, DC, MC, V
Children accepted
Disabled 1 room on ground floor
Pets accepted
Closed never
Proprietor Franco Maschietto

Santa Croce

Town hotel

Ai Due Fanali

A bas-relief of a saint inside the portico gives a clue to the hotel's origins as the *Scuola* of the Church of San Simeon Grande next door, in an elongated *campo* which is off the tourist track and soothingly crowd-free. By Venetian standards, this ancient building is quite unexceptional from the outside, but within, we found a glossy little hotel, stylishly furnished by its talented owner, Marina Ferron, who also owns the San Simeon Apartments (see page 142). The polished marble and stone floor of the ground-floor reception/sitting room is strewn with Persian rugs and dotted with fine antiques. The walls are hung with oil paintings and gilt-framed mirrors. Nick-nacks on the marble fireplace and fresh flowers create a homely feel .

There are great views from both the smart third-floor breakfast room (all green marble and wood) and the small roof terrace, perched on stilts on top of the building like a jetty out-of-water. Bedrooms are on the small side, but simply and tastefully decorated, with painted bedheads and modish stone-tiled bathrooms. All in all, this hotel provides Venetian sophistication without San Marco prices.

Nearby station; Scalzi; San Giacomo dell'Oro.

Campo San Simeon Grande,
Santa Croce 946, 30135 Venezia
Tel 041 718490
Fax 041 718344
E-mail request@aiduefanali.com
Website www.aiduefanali.com
Location across the Grand
Canal from the station;
vaporetto Ferrovia or water taxi
Meals breakfast
Prices LL
Rooms 17; 10 double and twin
and triple, 7 with bath, 3 with
shower; 7 single, 2 with bath, 5
with shower; all rooms have
phone, TV, air-conditioning,
minibar, hairdrier, safe
Facilities breakfast room, sitting
area, lift, roof terrace
Credit cards AE, DC, MC, V
Disabled possible, but no
special facilities .
Pets not accepted
Closed never
Proprietor Marina Ferron

49

Santa Croce

Town hotel

San Cassiano

Arriving by boat at San Cassiano's private jetty on the Grand Canal is considerably easier than finding your way by foot through a maze of tortuous, narrow alleyways from the nearest *vaporetto* or *traghetto* point (ask for a brochure to be sent so that you can follow its map). It also means that you can appreciate the 14thC *palazzo's* best feature: its deep red Gothic façade which faces the Grand Canal's greatest glory, the Ca' d'Oro. Inside, the hotel has a rather fusty feel to it, with heavy Venetian furnishings and a fairly lackadaisical staff – characteristics we also found in its sister hotels, the Marconi (page 44), the San Moisè (page 40) and the Ateneo (not included). Of the four, however, this one has the most grandiose rooms, and the six facing the canal are splendid, with capacious reproduction antique wardrobes, matching desks and carved bedheads, floating white curtains bordered by velvet or brocade pelmets, and oriental carpets. They are the same price as rooms without a view, and you should be tempted to look elsewhere if you can't secure one. The light, elegant breakfast room with huge windows and waterfront views is a delight.

Nearby Ca' d'Oro; Rialto Markets; Rialto Bridge.

Calle della Rosa, Santa Croce 2232, 30135 Venezia
Tel 041 5241768
Fax 041 721033
E-mail sancassiano@sancassiano.it
Website www.sancassiano.it
Location on Grand Canal, opposite Ca' d'Oro; **vaporetto** San Stae or water taxi
Meals breakfast
Prices LLL
Rooms 36; 20 double and twin, 12 triple and family, 4 single, all with bath or shower; all rooms have phone, TV, air-conditioning, minibar, hairdrier, safe
Facilities sitting room, breakfast room, bar
Credit cards AE, MC, V
Disabled 2 rooms specially adapted
Pets accepted
Closed never
Proprietor Franco Maschietto

Castello

Town hotel

Bisanzio

A recent inspection revealed a much improved lobby area, with white walls, beamed ceilings, twinkly halogen lights, marble floors, several separate sitting areas and a cosy bar. The furniture is still uniform: this is a straightforward tourist hotel. A new lift has been installed, and there is a large breakfast room, where a generous buffet is served. The big plus point here is the bedrooms, at least the good ones, which, as in many other Venice hotels, cost no more than the not-so-good ones. The latter are mainly dull boxes, while the former are light and airy bargains. Best are the eight rooms with private terraces and rooftop views. No. 34, for example, has a space-enhancing lobby leading to a bathroom tiled in pale green *corto Veneziano* tiles on one side, and on the other a large terrace with views of St Mark's *campanile*. No. 82 has a smaller terrace, but the room is large and light with a capacious bath and attractive marble basin (as are all the basins in this hotel). The rooms with double bed and bunk beds make an excellent choice for a family. Furnishings are mostly of the modern painted wood variety and floors and doors are insulated, cutting down outside noise to a minimum.
Nearby Riva degli Schiavoni; Piazza San Marco.

Calle de la Pietà, Castello 3651, 30122 Venezia
Tel 041 5203100
Fax 041 5204114
Location just off Riva degli Schiavoni, behind La Pietà
vaporetto San Zaccaria or by water taxi
Meals breakfast
Prices LLL
Rooms 43; 37 double, twin and triple, 2 single, 4 family, 20 with bath, 23 with shower; all rooms have phone, TV, air-

conditioning, minibar, hairdrier, safe
Facilities sitting room, bar, breakfast room, courtyard, lift
Credit cards AE, DC, MC, V
Disabled no special facilities
Pets accepted
Closed never
Proprietors Busetti family

Castello

Town guest-house

Bucintoro

We met a couple at Venice airport who had splashed out on the Londra Palace (which they liked very much) for the first few days of their stay and then sharply downgraded to the Bucintoro – which they almost preferred. Apart from the wonderful views across St Mark's Basin, which the two hotels share, the contrast could not be greater. Rooms at this basic *pensione*, little changed since the family bought it 30 years ago, are plain as a pikestaff; breakfast is frugal; and the sitting room, despite its newly upholstered armchairs, remains unappealing.

The secret of its success is its position: every clean and simple room has a lagoon view and is flooded with Venetian light. Corner rooms, beloved by artists, are the best, with windows on to both the lagoon and San Marco (try for Nos 1, 7, 9, 11). Room No. 4 is one of the pleasantest, with large bed, pretty bedspread, airy curtains and the waters of the lagoon gently lapping below. No. 26 can fit up to four people and has a fair-sized bathroom. The modest cement-rendered building with tables outside in summer is conveniently close to the Arsenale *vaporetto* stop.

Nearby Arsenale; Naval Museum; Piazza San Marco.

Riva San Biagio, Castello 2135, 30122 Venezia
Tel (041) 5223240
Fax (041) 5235224
Location on the waterfront, at the far end of Riva degli Schiavoni; vaporetto Arsenale, Tana or water taxi
Meals breakfast, dinner (Apr-Oct)
Prices LL
Rooms 28; 22 double, twin and triple, 17 with bath, 5 with shower; 6 single, 5 with shower, one with basin; all rooms have phone, fan on request, hairdrier
Facilities breakfast room, sitting room, terrace
Credit cards not accepted
Disabled not suitable
Pets not accepted
Closed Dec, Jan
Proprietor Bianchi family

Castello

Town hotel

Londra Palace

The position midway along the Riva is, of course, magnificent, with no less than 100 of the hotel's bedroom windows affording matchless views across the lagoon to the island of San Giorgio Maggiore with its perfect Palladian church of the same name. No wonder Tchaikovsky found it a congenial place in which to write his Fourth Symphony in 1877. Then there were two adjacent hotels, both opened in 1860; they merged in 1900, and now the Londra's costly refit, begun in 1992, has been completed, making it undoubtedly one of the premier hotels in the city. One of its best features now is that every room has been given the same lavish attention, so that you are unlikely to feel cheated by your allocation. The standard is high, and the quality of the Biedermeier furniture and the original paintings used throughout is exceptional. All the luxurious bathrooms have Jacuzzi baths. Rooms with views over the lagoon are termed 'deluxe' and are more expensive, but the 'superior' rooms without a view are equally rich in decoration. All are subtly different; some are really lovely. The public rooms are cool and chic and the terrace restaurant, Do Leoni, makes a romantic place in which to dine.
Nearby Piazza San Marco; San Giorgio in Bragora; San Zaccaria.

Riva degli Schiavoni,
30122 Venezia
Tel 041 5200533
Fax 041 5225032
E-mail info@hotelondra.it
Website www.hotelondra.it
Location midway along the waterfront, 2 mins walk from San Marco **vaporetto** San Zaccaria, San Marco
Meals breakfast, lunch, dinner
Prices LLLL
Rooms 53; 33 double and twin, 20 junior suites, all with bath;

all rooms have phone, TV, air-conditioning, minibar, hairdrier, safe, lift
Facilities sitting room, dining room, bar, terrace, sundeck, lift
Credit cards AE, DC, MC, V
Disabled no special facilities
Pets accepted
Closed never
Proprietor Ugo Samueli

Castello

Town hotel

Metropole

"We *love* this place" says the charming manager, Gianni de Rai. He and two colleagues still on reception joined the Metropole 28 years ago when it was bought by its current owner, Signor Beggiato. Between them they run one of the city's most idiosyncratic hotels, with a superb location, a high staff to guest ratio and much more personality than most places of this size. Everywhere you look – along corridors, on landings, in shelves and cupboards – are collections made by Signor Beggiato – angels, lecterns, church pews, corkscrews, crucifixes, cigarette cases and much more. The dignified decoration is faithful to the hotel's turn-of-the-century origins, but there are some eccentric flourishes. Room 251, for honeymooners, is wonderfully kitsch, with a bed surrounded by swirling marble pillars and gilt cherubs falling out of the ceiling. No.350 is another suite, altogether more sober and very cosy, with its own rooftop *altana* (balcony). The spacious breakfast room is a vision in candy pink and white, and the panelled and muralled little restaurant – serving an excellent buffet – is an intimate place in which to lunch or dine.
Nearby Piazza San Marco; San Zaccaria.

Riva degli Schiavoni, Castello 4149, 30122 Venezia
Tel 041 5205044
Fax 041 5223679
E-mail hotel.metropole@venere.it
Website www.venere.it/venezia/metropole
Location midway along the Riva, next to the church of La Pièta; vaporetto San Zaccaria, Arsenale or water taxi
Meals breakfast, lunch, dinner
Prices LLLL
Rooms 72; 56 double and twin, 3 single, 10 junior suites, 3 family; all rooms have phone, TV, air-conditioning, minibar, hairdrier, safe
Facilities breakfast room, dining room, sitting room, lift, garden
Credit cards AE, DC, MC, V
Disabled access possible
Pets accepted
Closed never
Proprietor Beggiato family

Castello

La Residenza

La Residenza appeals to true lovers of Venice who appreciate the chance to stay in the grand Gothic *palazzo* which dominates this dusty and enigmatic square, whose little church, San Giovanni in Bragora is one of the city's most appealing.

Just to enter is an experience: huge doors swing open to reveal an ancient covered courtyard and stone steps leading up to a vast Baroque hall with beautifully coloured, lavishly carved plaster walls. Taking breakfast here in the early morning light is a rare treat, though the hushed atmosphere can be oppressive. This, however, is not a grand hotel, but a modest two star in immodest surroundings. Those who appreciate the combination of grotty, kitsch and antique in the bedrooms will mourn the fact that half of them have been renovated (calm and pretty, but standard), and the rest are due for the same treatment. Perhaps Signor Ballestra will heed the pleas of his regulars and leave them alone. Then you can choose: old on the right or new on the left, the perfest solution.

By the way, the famous smell – of cats? or is it boiled cabbage? – seems to have retreated to the hallway.

Nearby San Giorgio degli Schiavoni; Arsenale.

Campo Bandiera e Moro, Castello 3608, 30122 Venezia
Tel 041 5285315
Fax 041 5238859
Location on small square 100 m behind Riva degli Schiavoni
vaporetto Arsenale, San Zaccaria
Meals breakfast
Prices LL
Rooms 14; 11 double and twin, 3 single, all with bath or shower; all rooms have phone, TV, air-conditioning, minibar

Facilities sitting room, breakfast area
Credit cards AE, MC, V
Disabled not suitable
Pets accepted
Closed never
Proprietor Giovanni Ballestra

Castello

Town-house apartments

Palazzetto San Lio

In this enigmatic, crumbly old house, skirted by canals, you can live out a Venetian fantasy amongst frescoed ceilings, silk covered walls, Murano glass chandeliers, rococo beds and antique painted Venetian furniture. The gaps are filled with unlovely sofas and lampstands and the eight apartments all have a genteel, slightly shabby air, which only adds to their romantic appeal. Perhaps the most charming is 'Affresco' on the *piano nobile*. In the reception room is the bed, screened off behind curtains. As depicted in paintings by Longhi, this was the custom, so that the lady of the house could receive guests in her boudoir, yet retire when she wished. The room is old fashioned and very Venetian, with an original frescoed ceiling. There is a tiny room with bunks, suitable for children, a simple kitchenette and an even simpler bathroom.

The house has a fine long entrance hall with original watergate. Here the family's gondola was kept. There is a marble staircase, antique mosaic on the landings, and, on the first floor, a tiny stuccoed chapel. New to the guide: readers' reports would be particularly welcome.

Nearby Campo Santa Maria Formosa; Rialto.

Contact Venetian Apartments, 413 Parkway House, Sheen Lane, London SW14 8LS
Tel 0181 878 1130
Fax 0181 878 0982
E-mail enquiries@venice-rentals.com
Website: www.venice-rentals.com
Location at the end of an alley off Salizzada San Lio between Rialto and Campo Santa Maria Formosa; vaporetto Rialto
Prices apartments from £450 to £899 per week (minimum rental one week); 'Affresco'

£650 per week
Rooms apartments range from studios to two bedrooms; all with kitchenette and bathroom; phone, heating
Disabled not suitable
Pets not accepted
Closed never

Castello

Town-house apartment

Venier

On the *piano nobile* of a16th-century house just off the delightful Campo Santa Maria Formosa, this amusing apartment is owned by the costume designer for Vienna State Opera and is suitably theatrical, colourful and indeed over-the-top, Venetian style. The mirrored entrance hall with Venetian chandeliers doubles as a dining room. The drawing room has brocade hangings, Venetian marble floor, Persian rugs, more mirrors and chandeliers and ornate furniture.

Two of the double bedrooms are particularly flamboyant – one with a huge hanging depicting Renaissance ladies and gentlemen playing at cards – although flamboyance is the keynote rather than luxury. The two bathrooms are enormous and there is a modern kichen and small single room. You can either rent the entire apartment, which sleeps up to seven, or, if it hasn't been previously let, you can take bed and breakfast (served in your room) for a minimum of two nights. In this case, take note that you will share a bathroom with other bed and breakfast guests. New to the guide: readers' reports would be particularly welcome.

Nearby Campo Santa Maria Formosa, Rialto.

Contact Veronica Tomasso Cotgrove, 10 St Mark's Crescent, London NW1
Tel (0171) 267 2423
Fax (0171) 267 4759
E-mail veronica.t.cotgrove@btinternet.com
Website www.btinternet.com/~veronica.t.cotgrove/vtc.htm
Location just off Campo Santa Maria Formosa; vaporetto Rialto
Prices apartment £1,650 per week (minimum rental one week); bed and breakfast rates also available
Rooms 3 double, one single bedroom, drawing room, dining room, two bathrooms, kitchen; telephone
Disabled not suitable
Pets not accepted
Closed never

Dorsoduro

Town hotel

Accademia

Though it's not the bargain it used to be, the Accademia still has affordable prices and a convenient but calm location. What really distinguishes the *pensione* is its gardens – the large canal-side patio, where tables are scattered among plants in classical urns, and the grassy rear garden where roses and fruit trees flourish.

Built in the 17thC as a private mansion, it retains touches of grandeur. Most of the furnishings are classically Venetian (the Murano chandeliers for once tasteful and harmonious), although the ground floor has recently been redecorated in a disappointingly bland style with the addition – to our inspector's horror – of automatic glass doors. Perfect for sitting and relaxing in is the thankfully unchanged and finely furnished first-floor landing. The airy breakfast room has crisp white tablecloths and a beamed ceiling; but, weather permitting, guests will inevitably opt to start their day in the garden. The bedrooms, renovated a few years ago to a high standard, have inlaid wooden floors and antiqued mirrors. Our inspector found some members of staff 'charming', but others 'churlish', though the latter don't seem to deter a loyal clientèle from returning here year after year.
Nearby Accademia gallery; Scuola Grande dei Carmini.

Fondamenta Bollani,
Dorsoduro 1058, 30123 Venezia
Tel 041 5210188/5237846
Fax 041 5239152
E-mail pensione.accademia@flashnet.it
Location where the Toletta and
Trovaso canals meet the Grand
Canal; **vaporetto** Accademia or
water taxi
Meals breakfast
Prices LL
Rooms 30; 22 double and twin,
9 with bath, 13 with shower; 7
single, 6 with shower; all rooms
have phone, TV; most have air-conditioning, hairdrier, safe
Facilities breakfast room, bar,
sitting room, garden
Credit cards AE, DC, MC, V
Disabled no special facilities
Pets accepted
Closed never
Proprietor Stefania Salmaso

Dorsoduro

Town guest-house

Agli Alboretti

The Alboretti is distinguished by its warm welcome, and genuine family atmosphere. Reception is a cosy wood-panelled room with paintings of Venice on the walls and a model of a 17thC galleon in its window; the ground-floor sitting room is small, but a second titting room on the first-floor makes a comfortable retreat (the TV is rarely used); the terrace behind the hotel, entirely covered by a pergola and set simply with tables and chairs, is a delight, especially for a leisurely breakfast in summer.

The style of the bedrooms is predominantly simple and modern, though a few rooms have an antique or two (such as No. 5). Like the rest of the hotel, they are well cared for and spotlessly clean, but the bathrooms, though totally renovated, are tiny, as are some of the rooms. None are large, but Nos 15, 18 and 22 are recommended for their garden view, and the former for its balcony on which you can breakfast.

Signora Linguerri runs a sophisticated restaurant next door, where you can eat in the pretty dining room or outside under the pergola; she is an expert on wine and her list offers an interesting selection.

Nearby Accademia gallery; Zattere; Gesuati.

Rio Terrà Foscarini, Dorsoduro 884, 30123 Venezia
Tel 041 5230058
Fax 041 5210158
E-mail alborett@gpnet.it
Location alongside the Accademia gallery; **vaporetto** Accademia
Meals breakfast, lunch, dinner
Prices LL
Rooms 20; 13 double and twin, 6 single, one family room, all with bath or shower; all rooms have phone, TV, air-condition-ing, hairdrier
Facilities sitting rooms, dining room, TV room, bar, terrace
Credit cards AE, MC, V
Disabled no special facilities
Pets accepted
Closed Jan occasionally; restaurant Wed, Thurs lunch
Proprietor Anna Linguerri

Dorsoduro

Town hotel

American

Set in a peaceful backwater of Dorsoduro, yet close to the Accademia and the Grand Canal, this is a quiet, dignified hotel with spacious reception rooms and a tiny terrace where you can take breakfast under a pergola in summer. The public areas have a sombre Edwardian air, with wood panelling and silk damask on the walls, tapestry or velvet upholstered chairs, Oriental rugs on Venetian mosaic floors, frilly white curtains and potted plants. Corridors are also panelled in wood, with little tables and chairs placed here and there. Bedrooms – some newly renovated – vary in size, as do the bathrooms, and though unexceptional they have pretty Venetian painted furniture (with minibars mercifully disguised as free-standing cupboards), ornate gilt mirrors and pretty Paisley-print bedspreads. Our reporter's bathroom had a black and white shower curtain covered in comical cats.

If you choose the American, you should do what you can to secure one of the nine bedrooms that overlook the canal. Nos 14 and 23 are particularly recommended, with three canal-facing French windows on two sides, and narrow balconies from where you can watch the water traffic drift by.

Nearby Accademia gallery; Zattere; Santa Maria della Salute.

Rio di San Vio, Dorsoduro 628, 30123 Venezia
Tel 041 5204733
Fax 041 5204048
E-mail hotameri@tin.it
Fax www.hotelamerican.com
Location midway along canal, which runs between Grand Canal and Giudecca Canal; **vaporetto** Accademia or water taxi
Meals breakfast
Prices LL
Rooms 28 double and twin and single, all with bath or shower; all rooms have phone, TV, air-conditioning, minibar, hairdrier, safe
Facilities sitting area, breakfast room, terrace
Credit cards AE, MC, V
Disabled no special facilities
Closed never
Proprietor Salvatore Sutera Sardo

Dorsoduro

Town hotel

La Calcina

The house where Ruskin lived is hard to resist, both for its histor-ical connection and for its location facing the sunny straits of the Giudecca canal. The simple *pensione*, inherited by a go-ahead young couple, has recently been given a facelift, and trans-formed into a stylish small hotel whose calm uncluttered rooms provide a welcome antidote to an excess of Venetian rococo. Attention to detail includes fresh flowers and classical music in the lobby, and incense in the bedrooms to clear stuffy smells.

Unlike many hotels in the city there is a marked difference in price between the rooms at the front with views across the glitter-ing water and the darkish back rooms, which have no view, but are equally comfortable. Most expensive are the corner rooms, where the sun streams in from two directions. None of the rooms is large, but all compensate with cool cream walls, warm parquet floors, antiques and gleaming bathrooms with heated towel rails. Breakfast is served in summer on the blue and white terrace (or you can book the romantic roof garden for two), and in winter in a marble-floored bar with a picture window, so that even if you opt for a bedroom at the back you can still enjoy the vista.
Nearby Gesuati church; Accademia gallery.

Fondamenta Zattere ai Gesuati, Dorsoduro 780, 30123 Venezia
Tel 041 5206466
Fax 041 5227045
Location on W side of San Vio canal; **vaporetto** Zattere or water taxi
Meals breakfast
Prices LL
Rooms 29; 22 double and twin, 2 with bath, 20 with shower; 7 single, 1 with bath, 3 with show-er, 3 with washbasin; all rooms have phone, air-conditioning, hairdrier, safe
Facilities breakfast room/bar, sitting area, terrace, roof terrace
Credit cards AE, DC, MC, V
Disabled not suitable
Pets not accepted
Closed never
Proprietors Alessandro and Debora Szemere

Dorsoduro

Town guest-house

Locanda Ca' Foscari

You will need help finding Calle Frescada, a little lane tucked almost out of sight and unmarked on most maps: take Calle Larga Foscari towards the Frari, and at the junction with Crosera, turn right. Calle Frescada runs across the end, and the hotel faces down Crosera. Happily our inspector's maddening search for this little one-star hotel was worth the effort – Ca' Foscari is a cut above. Somehow its charming, modest exterior – smart front door and bell pull, little lantern displaying its name – tells the story, and the interior does not disappoint, nor the welcome from Valter and Giuliana Scarpa.

On the ground floor is a little breakfast room. A couple of flights of stairs, and you are in a fresh, white corridor with white-painted doors leading to the bedrooms. These are modest, as you would expect, but pristine, with lacy curtains and pretty bed-spreads and white-tiled minute bathrooms, or, in rooms without bathrooms, decent basins. Note that the communal bathroom only has a shower, not a bath. The metal-framed beds are much more comfortable than they look. An excellent budget hotel in a bustling residential neighbourhood.

Nearby Scuola Grande di San Rocco; Frari; Accademia gallery.

Calle della Frescada, Dorsoduro 3888-3887/b, 30123 Venezia
Tel 041 710401/710817
Fax 041 710817
Location between Campo San Tomà and Palazzi Foscari; **vaporetto** San Tomà
Meals breakfast
Prices L
Rooms 11; 6 double and twin, 3 with shower, 3 with basin only; 1 single with shower; 2 triples without shower; 2 family rooms without shower; communal bathroom with shower
Facilities breakfast room
Credit cards MC, V
Disabled not suitable
Pets accepted
Closed 15 Nov to Feb
Proprietor Valter Scarpa

Dorsoduro

Apartments in private house

Palazzetto da Schio

Fondamenta Soranzo is a tranquil backwater lined with attractive houses, including this red-painted *palazzetto*, home of the da Schio family for the past 300 years. The present incumbent, Contessa da Schio, lives on the ground floor and *piano nobile* while other parts of the house have been converted into three charming and comfortable apartments, available from any period of time from two days to six months. Note, though, that the apartments are considerably less expensive when taken per week or per month, rather than per night. They are largely furnished with family antiques, including pictures and mirrors, with modern bits and pieces to fill the gaps. The topmost apartment (not for those who don't like stairs) has wide views and a large sitting room, while the rooms in the mezzanine apartment all face the canal. It has a cosy, antique-filled living room.

The entrance hall of the *palazzetto*, lit by precious Venetian torch lamps and opening on to the garden, is splendid. This, and the fine three-bedroom *piano nobile* apartment can be hired for parties at any time of the year and is available to stay in for one month in the summer.

Nearby Santa Maria della Salute; Accademia; Zattere.

Fondamenta Soranzo,
Dorsoduro 316/b, 30123
Venezia
Tel 041 5237937
Fax 041 5237937
E-mail avenezia@tin.it
Website www.web.tin.it/sangregorio
Location on canal between
Grand and Guidecca Canals;
vaporetto Salute or water taxi
Prices rates per night LL; rates
per week L-LL
Rooms 3 apartments, one with
one bedroom, 2 with 2 bed-

rooms; all with kitchen and
bathroom; phone; maid service
Credit cards AE, MC, V
Disabled not suitable
Pets not accepted
Closed never
Proprietor Contessa Anna da
Schio

Dorsoduro

Town hotel

Pausania

The San Barnaba area, traditionally the home of impecunious Venetian nobility, is quiet and picturesque, and now highly desirable as the better-known San Marco district becomes increasingly tourist-ridden and overpriced. The Pausania is a small hotel lying close to the last surviving floating vegetable shop in Venice – a colourful barge on the San Barnaba canal.

The building is quintessentially Venetian, a weathered Gothic *palazzo* with distinctive ogee windows. Inside, timbered ceilings, Corinthian columns, an ancient well-head and a battered but beautiful stone staircase are features of the original building. Bedrooms are all decorated in the same tastefully restrained style, combining restful blues and creamy yellows. A recent reporter complains of the lack of drawer space, but this is a problem common to many Venetian hotels. Breakfast is served in an airy modern extension overlooking a secluded garden. Unusually for such a small hotel, there are several comfortable places to sit, including a sunny canal-side landing with floor-to-ceiling windows, a beamy reception area and bar. Staff are cheerful and friendly.

Nearby Scuola Grande dei Carmini; Accademia gallery.

Fondamenta Gherardini, Dorsoduro 2824, 30123 Venezia
Tel 041 5222083
Fax 041 5222989
Location just W of Campo San Barnaba on San Barnaba canal; **vaporetto** Ca' Rezzonico or water taxi
Meals breakfast
Prices LL
Rooms 31; 23 double and twin, 3 single, 5 family, all with bath or shower; all rooms have phone, TV, air-conditioning, minibar, hairdrier
Facilities sitting room, bar, breakfast room, garden
Credit cards AE, MC, V
Disabled no special facilities, but some rooms on ground floor
Pets accepted
Closed never
Proprietor Guido Gatto

Dorsoduro

Town guest-house

Salute da Cici

A long-time favourite of ours, this calm, civilized hotel inhabits a *palazzo* on a small canal in an interesting area between the Accademia and Salute. If you've had your fill of baroque churches, it's also perfectly placed for a visit to the Guggenheim Collection and a blast of abstract expressionism.

The façade is charming and typically Venetian: peeling stucco and rose-coloured brick, Gothic windows and stone balconies decked with flowers. And the interior doesn't disappoint. It has a classically elegant lobby of columns and marble floors beneath exposed rafters. A little bar is reserved for guests, and a tiny, sheltered garden offers a few sunny tables for a drink. Interconnecting basement rooms, dating from the time when this was a *pensione*, provide breakfast areas. Corridors lead off a beautifully furnished first-floor landing to simple white-painted bedrooms with high ceilings, Venetian marble floors and furniture that ranges from antique to utility. There's no difference in price, so request a room on the canal or, if you're willing to sacrifice character for comfort, go for one of the nine modern rooms in the annexe.

Nearby Guggenheim Collection; Santa Maria della Salute.

Fondamenta di Ca' Balla ,
Dorsoduro 222, 30123 Venezia
Tel 041 5235404
Fax 041 5222271
Location just S of Rio Calle
Terra Nuovo, 5 mins walk E of
Salute; **vaporetto** Salute or
water taxi
Meals breakfast
Prices L
Rooms 50 double and twin,
single, triple and family, all with
bath or shower; all rooms have
phones

Facilities bar, sitting area,
breakfast room, garden
Credit cards not accepted
Disabled not suitable
Pets not accepted
Closed mid-Nov to Christmas,
Jan to Mar (or Carnival if
earlier)
Proprietor Sebastiano Cagnin

Dorsoduro

Town-house apartment

Salute Giallo

For the same daily rate as a standard room in a fairly simple hotel, this smart, sophisticated ground floor studio could be yours. Decorated and equipped to a high standard, it is a sophisticated vision in black and yellow: yellow tiled floor with black diamonds, yellow and black curtains, black bedcover with yellow stripes. The front door opens directly into this welcoming little home, with smart kitchenette immediately on the right, and a (black and yellow, of course) sofa bed on the left under a row of classical prints, with dining table in the centre. Beyond the sleeping area is a compact but newly fitted bathroom, and a tiny enclosed courtyard. This is a perfect apartment for a couple, or even a small family.

There are three other apartments in the building, all decorated and furnished to the same standard, the larger ones having lovely furniture and *objects d'art*. With their beamed ceilings, white walls, open fires and painted ceramics, they have a decidedly Tuscan feel. The house is in a quiet residential side street and you will soon feel part of the neighbourhood. New to the guide: readers' reports are particularly welcome.

Nearby Salute; Accademia gallery; Zattere.

Contact Venetian Apartments, 413 Parkway House, Sheen Lane, London SW14 8LS
Tel (0181) 878 1130
Fax (0181) 878 0982
E-mail enquiries@venice-rentals.com
Website www.venice-rentals.com
Location in a side street between Accademia and Salute; vaporetto Salute
Prices apartments from £499 to £875 per week (minimum rental one week); 'Giallo' £550 per week

Rooms apartments comprise 2 studios and 2 one-bedroom, sleeping 2-4 people; all have kitchen, bathroom, phone, TV
Disabled access possible
Pets not accepted
Closed never

Dorsoduro

Town guest-house

Seguso

Sitting on the wide sunny promenade of the Zattere, lapped by the choppy waters of the wide Giudecca canal, gives you the distinct feeling of being by the seaside. This open setting, with a grand panorama across the lagoon, is just one of the charms of the Seguso. A *pensione* in the old tradition, it is family-run, friendly and solidly old-fashioned. And (unlike most hotels in Venice) prices are modest; the Seguso is not noted for its food, but half-board here costs no more than bed and breakfast alone in hotels of similar comfort closer to San Marco.

The best bedrooms are the large ones at the front of the house, overlooking the canal – though for the privilege of the views and space you may have to forfeit the luxury of a private bathroom (only half the rooms have their own facilities). The main public rooms are the dining room, prettily furnished in traditional style, and the modest sitting room where you can sink into large leather chairs and peruse ancient editions of travel writing and guidebooks. Breakfast is taken on the front terrace – delightful. Fellow guests are often friendly, interesting and great Venice enthusiasts.

Nearby Accademia gallery; Gesuati church.

Zattere ai Gesuati, Dorsoduro 779, 30123 Venezia
Tel 041 5222340/5286858
Fax 041 5222340
Location 5 mins walk S of Accademia, overlooking Giudecca canal; **vaporetto** Zattere or water taxi
Meals breakfast, lunch, dinner
Prices LL
Rooms 36; 31 double and twin, 5 single, 9 with bath, 9 with shower; all rooms have phone
Facilities dining room, sitting room, lift, terrace
Credit cards AE, MC, V
Disabled access possible
Pets accepted
Closed Dec to Feb
Proprietors Seguso family

Cannaregio

Town bed-and-breakfast

Club Cristal

The setting could hardly be more ideal, at least for those seeking a peaceful backwater: an airy, palatial town house overlooking a tree-lined courtyard and a little canal in a quiet residential corner of Cannaregio, yet only five minutes' walk from the Ca' d'Oro. It is the family home of Susan Schiavon, an Englishwoman ("not *pure* English; lots of other nationalities come into it besides") who has lived in Venice for many years and now lets five of its bedrooms to discerning visitors for whom she is a fund of knowledge about the city.

An elegant white marble staircase leads to the *piano nobile* and a high-ceilinged sitting room filled with books and squashy sofas and armchairs. A perfect breakfast is served on the plant-filled terrace beyond. The bedrooms, entered through original doors painted with birds and flowers, vary in size, some large; all are full of character, with family furniture, comfortable beds, and crisp linen. Susan serves dinner by arrangement, and you should take advantage of her accomplished home cooking at least once. Take note that Club Cristal is emphatically a home, not a hotel; couples often return, and lone women feel particularly at ease. **Nearby** Gesuiti; Ca' d'Oro; Rialto.

For further information all nationalities should contact: Liz Heavenstone, 188 Regent's Park Road, London NW1 8XP, England **Tel** (London) 0171 722 5060 **Fax** 0171 586 3004 **E-mail** susan.venice@iol.it **Location** on a small canal, between Ca' d'Oro; and Gesuiti **vaporetto** Ca' d'Oro, Fondamente Nuove **Meals** breakfast, dinner by arrangement **Prices** rooms (payable to London office in sterling only) £50–£125; standard double £80–£125; single night supplement; dinner £25 (including wine); breakfast included **Rooms** 4 double, 1 single, all with bath or shower; all rooms have hairdrier **Facilities** sitting room, dining room, terrace **Credit cards** AE, D **Disabled** not suitable **Pets** not accepted **Closed** never **Proprietor** Susan Schiavon

Cannaregio

Town hotel

Giorgione

If you're coming to Venice with teenage children, this comfortable four-star could be an excellent choice. When sight-seeing begins to pall, they can retreat to the pool table or the well-equipped games room. Unlike many Venetian hotels, there is plenty of sitting space downstairs, a cosy bar and large secluded garden with a pond and no shortage of tables and chairs. The occasional column, arch and exposed beam are reminders that this is a 15thC *palazzo*, although bland decoration doesn't always make the best of these features. Silk damask swagged curtains and upholstered sofas and chairs furnish the public rooms; while many of the bedrooms look twee and dated.

Some of the standard double rooms are on the small side, so for an extra 50.000L, opt for a superior or, better still, for another 50.000L for one of the 'loft suites', tucked into the eaves with its own terrace, where you can eat a lazy breakfast or sip a Prosecco at sunset, the rooftops of the city spread out before you. Breakfast downstairs is a generous buffet of fruit, cereal, rolls, salami and eggs, served in a large white room decorated with bad frescoes. New to the guide.

Nearby Santi Apostoli; Miracoli; Ca' d'Oro.

Santi Apostoli, Cannaregio
4587, 30131 Venezia
Tel 041 5225810
Fax 041 5239092
E-mail giorgione@hotelgiorgione.com
Website www.hotelgiorgione.com
Location just off Campo Santi
Apostoli to the north; vaporetto
Ca' d'Oro
Meals breakfast
Prices LLL
Rooms 70; 60 double and twin
and single, 10 suites, all with
bath; all rooms have phone, TV,
air-conditioning, minibar, hair-
drier
Facilities sitting areas, breakfast
room, games room, bar, lift,
garden
Credit cards AE, DC, MC, V
Disabled access possible
Pets not accepted
Closed never
Manager Signor Zanolin

Cannaregio

Town hotel

Locanda Ai Santi Apostoli

Be on the lookout for a pair of handsome dark green doors which herald the discreet entrance of this converted *palazzo*. Beyond is a scruffy courtyard and a quirky lift that takes you up to the third floor. What lies in store for you here is totally unexpected: a lovely apartment that has been transformed by the Bianchi Michiel family into an elegant, if pricey, B&B. The sitting room is the epitome of style: oil paintings hang on glossy apricot walls; heavy lamps rest on antique tables; sofas and chairs are covered in quiet chintz or swathed in calico. At the far end, a triptych of wood-framed windows overlooks the Grand Canal. Ornaments and books left casually around make it feel more like a home than a hotel.

Large and individually decorated, the bedrooms have been done out recently in glazed chintzes and stunning strong colours. Like the sitting room, they are dotted with antiques and pretty china nick-nacks. The two on the Grand Canal are considerably dearer than the rest. Stefano also owns a one-bedroom apartment on the second floor, with a vibrant green colour scheme, no view of the canal, but a sunny roof terrace.

Nearby Ca' d'Oro; Santi Apostoli; Miracoli.

Strada Nova, Cannaregio 4391, 30131 Venezia
Tel 041 5212612
Fax 041 5212611
Location just E of Campo Santi Apostoli; **vaporetto** Ca' d'Oro
Meals breakfast
Prices LLL; apartment prices on request
Rooms 11 double and twin, 6 with bath, 4 with shower; all rooms have phone, TV, air-conditioning, minibar, hairdrier

Facilities breakfast room, sitting room, lift
Credit cards AE, DC, MC, V
Disabled not suitable
Pets accepted
Closed Jan to mid-Feb, 2–3 weeks in Aug, sometimes 2 weeks in Dec
Proprietor Stefano Bianchi Michiel

Cannaregio

Locanda Leon Bianco

Hidden away in an enclosed courtyard, behind a sturdy door in the wall, and approached by stone steps rising up a cavernous brick-walled stairwell, we discovered this gem. Recently opened by the owner of La Galleria, Luciano Benedetti (see page 143) and two friends, the locanda occupies one floor of an old *palazzo* and has a reception area and seven large, attractive bedrooms with small, modern bathrooms. Once upstairs, the only signs of the building's age are undulating floors – some marble, some parquet – and immense tilted wooden doors. There is a kitchen but no breakfast room, so breakfast is served in the bedrooms.

Three of the bedrooms boast that most sought-after of Venetian views: over the Grand Canal. They are furnished simply but tastefully with a mix of antiques and pretty painted furniture, and freshly decorated in pale colours with cherubs frescoed on the ceilings. A more dramatic fresco is emblazoned across one wall of a huge bedroom on the street side. Although the Leon Bianco doesn't offer the services or address of the ritzy San Marco hotels, prices – 250,000L per night for a double room on the Grand Canal — are irresistible by comparison.

Nearby Santi Apostoli; Miracoli; Rialto.

Corte Leon Bianco, Cannaregio
5629, 30131 Venezia
Tel 041 5233572
Fax 041 2416392
E-mail leonebi@tin.it
Location in courtyard between
Santi Apostoli and Santa
Giovanni Crisostomo canals;
vaporetto Ca' d'Oro, Rialto
Meals breakfast
Prices L-LL
Rooms 7; 6 double and twin
with shower, one family with
bath; all rooms have phone

Facilities none
Credit cards AE, DC, MC, V
Disabled not suitable
Pets not accepted
Closed never
Proprietors Luciano Benedetti,
Stefano Franceschini, Claudio
Novo

Cannaregio

Town hotel

Locanda di Orsaria

In a street with its fair share of hotels, the Locanda di Orsaria is by far the smallest and by far the most charming. The front door, flanked by bay trees, leads straight into a pretty, beamed reception-cum-breakfast room, which, though the size of a shoebox, seats 12 for a slap-up buffet breakfast each morning. Wooden furniture, fresh flowers and a tapestry hung on a wall lend a country air, echoed upstairs in the simply, yet tastefully furnished bedrooms. We were amazed and pleased by their size in comparison with the ground floor. The windows are big too, and – of great significance in summer – this is the only hotel in Venice, the owner claims, where all the rooms have mosquito screens. Terracotta floors and white-painted walls, both upstairs and down, loose-weave chintz bedspreads, and attractive plain wood furniture (we loved the 'dressing chests') mark the style as more Tuscan than Venetian.

Since the retirement of the ebullient Renato Polesel, a larger than life character who presided over this diminutive gem for a number of years, Pietro, his equally friendly and helpful son, has been running the hotel.

Nearby station; Scalzi; Palazzo Labia; San Geremia.

Calle Priuli, Cannaregio 103, 30121 Venezia
Tel 041 715254
Fax 041 715433
E-mail orsaria@iol.it
Website www.venezialberghi.com
Location next to the station, to the E; **vaporetto** Ferrovia
Meals breakfast
Prices LL
Rooms 8; 5 double and twin, 3 triple, all with shower; all rooms have phone, TV, air-conditioning, minibar, hairdrier, safe
Facilities breakfast room
Credit cards AE, DC, MC, V
Disabled 1 room on ground floor
Pets accepted
Closed 3 weeks at beginning of Dec
Proprietor Pietro Polesel

Lagoon Islands

Village hotel, Lido

Ca' del Borgo

If you are looking for somewhere calm and refined in which to install a group of friends, Ca' del Borgo could be an answer; as well as operating as an ordinary hotel, it is particularly well suited to private parties.

Ca' del Borgo stands in a wide, quiet street in Malamocco. A handsome town house, it was renovated a few years ago for private use, and then sold to the present hotelier owners. It retains the air of a gracious and civilized home, with eight spacious, comfortable and smartly decorated bedrooms with a large terrace and a little garden with a stone well. A grandiose entrance hall with beamed ceiling and oriental rugs sets the tone. Bedrooms have parquet floors, oriental rugs, excellent beds, perhaps deep red silk damask on the walls, perhaps a colour scheme of yellow and blue. Bathrooms are marble, with efficient showers. Service is discreet.

A car would be useful. The hotel is out of the way, and it could transport guests to the Ca' del Moro sports and health club, which they are entitled to use; they also have use of the Hotel Excelsior's beach. Free bikes are provided.

Nearby Venice; Lagoon Islands.

Piazza delle Erbe, Malamocco, Lido, 30126 Venezia
Tel 041 770749
Fax 041 770799
E-mail mabapa@venicehotel.com
Website www.venicehotel.com/mabapa
Location in Malamocco village, 6 km SW of Lido; parking
vaporetto Santa Maria Elisabetta then taxi or hotel minibus, or by hotel water taxi
Meals breakfast
Prices LL
Rooms 8 double and twin, 3 with bath (2 with jacuzzi bath), 5 with shower; all rooms have phone, TV, air-conditioning, minibar, hairdrier, safe
Facilities sitting room, breakfast room, terrace; catering facilities available
Credit cards AE, DC, MC, V
Disabled one specially adapted room on ground floor
Pets accepted
Closed Dec, Jan
Proprietor Signor Vianello

Lagoon Islands

Restaurant-with-rooms, Torcello

Locanda Cipriani

We do not apologize for including the Locanda Cipriani, even though its rooms are, as we write, closed, and may never open again. A planning dispute has caused the problem, but we hope that by the time you read this they are once more open, because they are amongst the loveliest in this guide. In the meantime, you can still eat in the restaurant, or out on the terrace in fine weather, although on our visits we found the prices high.

Torcello is the cradle of the Venetian civilization, yet all that remains are two serenely beautiful churches, Santa Fosca and the ancient cathedral, the last with its haunting Byzantine mosaic of the Madonna. When the crowds drift home, Torcello's magic begins to work, and only the Locanda's guests are privileged to witness it. These have included Hemingway, Chaplin and Paul Newman, while the entire British royal family has lunched here. The rooms are simple and homely yet sophisticated, with polished wood floors, attractive pictures on white walls, writing desks, *objets d'art*, comfortable sofas and armchairs. As the owner, grandson of its founder Harry Cipriani, says, their closure would be a loss to Venice.

Nearby Venice (40 mins); Lagoon Islands.

Torcello, 30012 Burano, Venezia
Tel 041 730150
Fax 041 735433
Location in centre of island, overlooking the cathedral; **vaporetto** Torcello
Meals breakfast, lunch, dinner
Prices on application
Rooms 6; 3 double with sitting rooms, 3 single, all with bath; all rooms have phone
Facilities sitting room, dining room, bar, terrace, garden

Credit cards AE, MC, V
Disabled not suitable
Pets accepted
Closed Nov to mid-Mar
Proprietor Bonifacio Brass

Lagoon Islands

Seaside hotel, Lido

Quattro Fontane

The longer we lingered at the Quattro Fontane, the more it grew on us. At first the 150-year-old mock Tyrolean building struck us as rather gloomy and suburban, but we soon warmed to the charmingly decorated reception rooms, particularly the *salone* and the little writing room. Mementos of the owners' travels are dotted around the hotel on walls and shelves – carved wooden figures, painted shells, model ships, porcelain, stamps. In the baronial dining room, with its cavernous hearth and bold red chairs, service was directed with courtesy by the long-serving head waiter. In warm weather you can eat on the wide tree-filled terrace that encircles the hotel.

The bedrooms in the main building have plenty of character and are individually decorated with an assortment of furniture, pictures and fabrics, comfortable if not luxurious. Those in the 1960s annexe are more streamlined, but here too each is different, attractive and cosy, with gaily tiled bathrooms. A dignified hotel, elderly now, but still spruce, and in our opinion the best on the Lido. Only giggling, secretly smoking chambermaids let the side down on our visit.

Nearby Venice; Lagoon Islands.

Via Quattro Fontane 16,
30126 Lido, Venezia
Tel 041 5260227
Fax 041 5260726
Location set back from seafront
on S side of Lido, near Casino;
vaporetto Santa Maria
Elisabetta
Meals breakfast, lunch, dinner
Prices LLL
Rooms 58; 54 double, 4 single,
35 with bath, 23 with shower; all
rooms have phone, TV, air-
conditioning, hairdrier, safe

Facilities sitting room, writing
room, dining room, bar; tennis
court and beach cabins
available
Credit cards AE, DC, MC, V
Disabled access difficult
Pets accepted
Closed Nov to Easter
Proprietor Bevilacqua family

Lagoon Islands

Restaurant-with-rooms, Burano

Al Raspo de Ua

If you want an interesting experience, local colour, and indeed charm at probably the lowest price in the Venetian Lagoon, then this could be it. And Venice is only a 40-minute *vaporetto* ride away.(The photograph shows Burano's waterfront.)

Al Raspo de Ua is a restaurant at the heart of the meltingly pretty island of Burano, with its brightly daubed little houses, on a pedestrian thoroughfare, close to a canal. To be truthful, it is flanked by souvenir shops and picture postcard stands, but the restaurant itself is bustling and well turned out, clearly the most popular on the island, packed at lunchtime in season. The back room, hung with fishing nets, has its share of character, and the staff, when we visited, seemed to be good types.

When evening comes, and the day trippers depart to the city, the charm should start to work its spell. This is no more, or less, than a simple restaurant with rooms to let above (the only facility for lodgers, apart from the bedrooms, is a separate side entrance for their use) but the rooms are cheerful enough, clean, and fairly recently equipped, with just one communal bathroom. This place is a well-kept secret: make sure you book well ahead.
Nearby Venice; Lagoon Islands.

Via Galuppi 560, Burano, 30012 Venezia
Tel 041 730095
Fax 041 730397
Location at centre of island, on pedestrian thoroughfare, 5 mins walk from landing stage; **vaporetto** Burano
Meals breakfast, lunch, dinner
Prices L
Rooms 5 double; one communal bathroom with shower only, plus one further WC

Facilities dining room, sitting area
Credit cards AE, DC, MC, V
Disabled not suitable
Pets accepted
Closed Jan; restaurant closed Wed
Proprietors Mario Bruzzese and Giuliano Padouan

✦ *Lagoon Islands*

Seafront hotel, Lido

Villa Mabapa

Set peacefully in a garden overlooking the lagoon, Villa Mabapa
is one of the Lido's most popular hotels, although in the past
our inspectors have been less than enthusiastic, criticising the
cool, dismissive attitude of the reception staff and management,
the dowdy decoration and the banal food.

The hotel now consists of three buildings. The Villa itself, built
as a family home in the 1930s, contains the high-ceilinged public
rooms and some traditional-style bedrooms. The best are on the
first floor. Our inspector reports that hers, although a lovely
room with a huge sweep of windows overlooking the lagoon, was
haphazardly furnished and felt rather bare. The bedrooms in the
annexe, although recently redecorated, are dull, and all the
same. The hotel has recently acquired the villa next door, where
nine further rooms are available. At the rear of the main hotel is
a garden which is overlooked by the dining room, but the best
place to eat is on the terrace, with wonderful sunset views.

And the name? It consists of the first syllables of the words
mamma, bambino, and *papà.* These days, it is the *bambino* who is in
charge.

Nearby Venice; Lagoon Islands.

Riviera San Nicolò 16, Lido,
30126 Venezia
Tel 041 5260590
Fax 041 5269441
Location on Lagoon side of the
Lido, 15 mins walk from Santa
Maria Elisabetta landing stage;
in gardens; parking **vaporetto**
San Nicolò (infrequent stop),
Santa Maria Elisabetta or by
water taxi
Meals breakfast, lunch, dinner
Prices LLL **Rooms** 69; 53
double and twin, 15 single, 1

suite, all with bath or shower;
all rooms have phone, TV, air-
conditioning, hairdrier, safe
Facilities sitting room, breakfast
room, dining room, bar, lift,
terrace, garden
Credit cards AE, DC, MC, V
Disabled some rooms on
ground floor
Pets accepted
Closed sometimes Jan
Proprietor Signor Vianello

Veneto

Country villa, Arcugnano

Villa Michelangelo

Much of the southern Veneto countryside is flat and industrial-ized and the undulating vine-clad slopes of Monte Berico make not only a pleasant contrast but also an attractive central base for visiting Verona, Padua and Vicenza. Villa Michelangelo has the further advantage of a peaceful setting, wide views and a pool with sliding glass roof overlooking the Berici hills.

The severe-looking 18thC villa was formerly a Capuchin college before it became a hotel, and there is a simplicity about its decorative style even now. The dining room is elegant, with white walls, sparkling white Murano glass chandeliers suspended from a roughly beamed ceiling, a wall of glass doors leading to the terrace, and great vases of perfumed flowers. The food served here is fancy Italian which doesn't always come off. Bedrooms are fairly uniform, comfortable enough but unmemo-rable. The bathrooms have large green marble basins and proper towels.

Reached from the lobby by a tunnel, the conference centre, along with the pool and piano bar, is cleverly positioned so that the tranquillity of the hotel remains undisturbed.

Nearby Vicenza (7 km); Verona (40 km); Padua (40 km).

Via Sacco 19, 36057 Arcugnano, Vicenza
Tel 0444 550300
Fax 0444 550490
E-mail reception@hotelvillamichelangelo.com
Website www.hotelvillamichelangelo.com
Location 7 km S of Vicenza, signposted from Arcugnano, in own park with ample parking
Meals breakfast, lunch, dinner
Prices LL
Rooms 54; 34 double and twin, 15 single, 2 family, 3 suites, all with bath or shower; all rooms have phone, TV, air-conditioning, minibar, hairdrier
Facilities dining room, piano bar, terrace, pool, conference room, lift
Credit cards AE, DC, MC, V
Disabled two rooms specially adapted **Pets** accepted
Closed never
Manager Sebastiano Leder

Veneto

Town hotel, Asolo

Al Sole

From a glorious position, perched above the Piazza Maggiore on the steep hill up to the massive fortress, the Rocca, this *albergo* has a splendid view of the medieval town with its higgledy-piggledy streets. Its deep pink façade is original and appealing, while the trendy interior – hallmark of the dynamic young owner Silvia de Checchi – affords a dramatic contrast.

Almost every room has white rough-cast walls and mellow wood floors, enlivened by daring colour combinations for fabrics and furniture. Although the look is mainly cool and modern, a few antiques and the occasional bowl and pitcher hark back to the past. Recalling former stars in Asolo's firmament, such as 'Eleanor Duse' and 'Gabriele D'Annunzio', the bedrooms are all different; the former has light painted furniture, the latter, ornate church-style pieces. Some rooms have huge claw-foot baths; some have massage showers, just one of the many four-star comforts. Perhaps the ultimate of these is the state-of-the-art downstairs lavatory, which electronically flushes, lifts and then replaces the seat, complete with hygenic paper cover, at the appropriate times.

Nearby Palladian villas; Possagno (10 km).

Via Collegio 33, 31011 Asolo, Treviso
Tel 0423 528111
Fax 0423 528399
E-mail albergoalsole@sevenonline.it
Website
www.sevenonline.it/albergoalsole
Location at the top of Piazza Maggiore; private car park
Meals breakfast
Prices LL
Rooms 23; 14 double and twin, 2 with bath, 12 with shower; 8 single, 2 with bath, 6 with shower; 1 suite with bath; all rooms have phone, TV, air-conditioning, minibar, hairdrier, safe
Facilities breakfast room, sitting room, sitting area, bar, meeting room, lift, terrace
Credit cards AE, MC, V
Disabled 2 specially adapted rooms
Pets accepted
Closed never
Proprietor Silvia de Checchi

Veneto

Country Villa, Asolo

Villa Cipriani

Asolo is a beautiful medieval hilltop village commanding panoramic views, a jewel of the Veneto. The Villa Cipriani, a jewel of the huge ITT Sheraton Group, is a mellow ochre-washed house on the fringes of the village, its deceptively plain entrance leading into a warm reception area which immediately imparts the feeling of a hotel with a heart (and a house with a past: it was once the home of Robert Browning). Today it is graced by the prettiest of rose-and-flower-filled gardens, and meals are served on the terrace or in the restaurant over-hanging the valley. As for the gracious and comfortable bed-rooms, make sure you ask for one with a view, and try for an 'exclusive' rather than a 'superior' double. The latter are not particularly spacious, while the former include a sitting area; two rooms have terraces.

Villa Cipriani is a relaxing country hotel, whose views, comfort, peaceful garden and good food make it particularly alluring. However, some reports complain of prices that were hard to justify, also mentioning intrusive wedding parties and brash clientele. Others have been full of praise.

Nearby Palladian villas; Possagno (10 km).

Via Canova 298, 31011 Asolo, Treviso
Tel 0423 952166
Fax 0423 952095
E-mail gianpaolo_burattin@sheraton.com
Website www.sheraton.com/villacipriani
Location on NW side of village; with garage parking
Meals breakfast, lunch, dinner
Prices LLL-LLLL
Rooms 31; 29 double and twin, 2 single, all with bath; all rooms have phone, TV, air-conditioning, minibar, hairdrier
Facilities sitting room, dining rooms, bar, meeting room, lift, terrace, garden
Credit cards AE, DC, MC, V
Disabled access difficult
Pets accepted
Closed never
Manager Gianpaolo Burattin

Veneto

Agriturismo, Barbarano

Il Castello

Il Castello refers to a handsome villa built in the 17thC on the ruins of an ancient castle which looks down over the medieval village of Barbarano. Occupied for the last century by the Marinoni family, it retains the original perimeter walls of the castle, and its cellars. There is a Renaissance garden and a citrus garden, the lemon trees standing in rows of terracotta pots. To the south stretches the family's vineyard; *grappa*, olive oil and honey are also produced.

As you enter Il Castello through stone gates and a cobbled, covered way, the family villa is on the right, and the guest house ahead, overlooking a large walled courtyard. Adjacent is a converted barn, used for concerts, exhibitions and wedding parties; guests can meet and chat here if they like.

There are four separate apartments, for which reservations must be made on a weekly basis,.each sleeping up to five people, and all with fully equipped kitchens and bathrooms. Rooms, white-painted and airy, with Venetian marble floors, are somewhat spartan in feel, despite the use of old family furniture throughout. English is spoken.

Nearby Vicenza (22 km); Padua (32 km); Verona (34 km).

Via Castello 6, 36021
Barbarano, Vicenza
Tel 0444 886055
Fax 0444 886055
E-mail ilcastello@tin.it
Location on S side of
Barbarano; follow signs to Il
Castello in village; in own
grounds with secure parking
Meals none
Prices L; heating extra
Rooms two apartments with
kitchen and bathroom each
sleeping up to 6 people

Facilities garden, produce shop
Credit cards not accepted
Disabled access possible
Closed never
Proprietor Elda Marinoni and
family

Veneto

Seafront hotel, Chioggia

Grande Italia

Getting to this lively port on a spit of land 35 km south of Venice is not easy – a 50-minute drive from Venice on the mainland or an hour and a half's journey by boat and bus from the Lido via Pellestrina – but it's well worth the effort. One of Chioggia's attractions is the morning fish market on the Canale delle Vena (daily except Mon); another is its porticoed main street, the Corso del Popolo, lined with colourful shops and restaurants (including the excellent seafood restaurant El Gatto).

The Grande Italia has a perfect situation, at the junction of the Corso and the lagoon, with the best – and most expensive – rooms offering a view of one or the other. It's fun to watch the people in the Corso, but to see the sun rise through the mist above the endless expanse of calm water is magical. The 1914 building has a handsome exterior and a few internal details that have escaped a recent refurbishment intact – a red-carpeted wrought-iron staircase, cornicing, decorated ceilings and an airy breakfast room with wooden doors, marble floor and chandeliers. Though comfy and well-equipped, bedrooms are disappointingly uniform. New to the guide.

Nearby Lagoon Islands; Venice; Padua.

Rione San Andrea 599, 130015 Chioggia
Tel 041 400515
Fax 041 400185
Location on the lagoon, opposite the ferry terminal; with private parking
Meals breakfast, lunch, dinner
Prices L-LL
Rooms 57; 49 double and twin, 8 suites, all with bath; all rooms have phone, TV, air conditioning, minibar, hairdrier, safe
Facilities sitting area, breakfast room, restaurant, meeting room, gym, sauna, lift
Credit cards AE, DC, MC, V
Disabled special bathrooms on every floor
Pets accepted
Closed never
Manager Dora Gazza

Veneto

Town hotel, Cortina d'Ampezzo

Menardi

Old black-and-white photographs are evidence of how this family-run hotel on the northern side of Cortina has evolved. Built as a home in 1836 on the main highway connecting the Kingdom of Italy with the Hapsburg Empire, it became a coaching inn when its owners, the Menardi family, began hiring out horses and then providing rough and ready accommodation for weary travellers. During the First World War, Luigi Menardi found himself working as a porter in a Florence hotel, and when he returned to the mountains, began to transform the rustic inn into a proper hotel. Today the long white building has proliferated carved green wood balconies and tumbling geraniums, plus an extra line of rooms sprouting from the roof and a separate annexe behind, but the Menardi family can still justifiably proclaim: 'same house, same family, same relaxed atmosphere'. Inside, antique pieces, painted religious statues and old work tools are mixed with local custom-made furnishings which look somewhat dated but are nonetheless comfortable. The atmosphere is one of traditional warmth and service is polished. The large garden is a secluded delight.

Nearby skiing; Dolomites; Belluno (71 km).

Via Majon 110, 32043 Cortina d'Ampezzo, Belluno
Tel 0436 2400
Fax 0436 862183
E-mail hmenardi@sunrise.it
Website www.sunrise.it/cortina/alberghi/menardi
Location on SS51, on northern side of Cortina; in large grounds with private parking
Meals breakfast, lunch, dinner
Prices LL
Rooms 51 double and twin, single and family rooms, all with bath; all rooms have phone, TV, hairdrier
Facilities sitting room, dining room, bar, garden
Credit cards AE, DC, MC, V
Disabled access difficult
Pets not accepted
Closed Oct to mid-Dec, mid-Apr to mid-Jun
Proprietors Menardi family

Veneto

Self-catering Palladian villa, Finale

Villa Saraceno

Highlights of the Veneto are the villas built by the great Renaissance architect Andrea Palladio. If you would like to stay in one, here is your chance. Villa Saraceno, on a plain to the west of the Euganean Hills, is owned by the Landmark Trust, a British organization which acquires and restores buildings of historic interest and then lets them to holidaymakers.

Designed in the mid-16thC as a country retreat as well as working farm for a well-to-do Vicenzan, Biagio Saraceno, the complex consists of the airy, beautifully proportioned main house as well as other earlier buildings, including the simple Casa Vecchia, in which most of the bedrooms are located. The interior of the Palladian house has been restored to recreate its original arrangement – a grand *sala* with two-room apartments opening off it and huge granaries above. Dim frescoed friezes have been cleaned to reveal scenes of high drama, probably painted for Biagio's son. Saraceno can accommodate up to 16 people. One recent tenant wrote to the Landmark Trust: 'a perfect balance between the elegant understatement of the Palladian building and modern-day comforts ... '

Nearby Montagnana (14 km); Vicenza (32 km).

Via Finale 8, 36020 Agugliaro, Vicenza. For all information and booking contact: The Landmark Trust, Shottesbrooke, Maidenhead, Berkshire SL6 3SW, England **Tel** 01628 825925 **Fax** 01628 825417 (Landmark Trust) **E-mail** booking@landmarktrust.co.uk **Website** www.landmarktrust.co.uk **Location** in village 32 km S of Vicenza, 12 km N of SS10 between Este and Montagnana **Meals** none **Prices** weekly rates for villa from £1,200 to £5,700 depending on dates; weekly lets only in high season, shorter stays available at other times **Rooms** accommodates up to 16 in 2 double, 3 twin, 2 single, 1 family room; 5 bathrooms **Facilities** kitchen with dishwasher and washing machine, sitting room, dining room, garden, swimming pool **Credit cards** MC, V **Disabled** access difficult **Pets** accepted **Closed** never

Veneto

Town hotel, Follina

Abbazia

The hotel consists of two buildings: a 17thC *palazzo* and, adjacent, an enchanting little art nouveau villa. Standards of decoration and comfort in both are exceptionally high – rarely have we met hoteliers (brother and sister) more keen to please their guests. If you find the lobby and balconied breakfast area a bit much – a sugary pink confection of candy-striped walls strewn with roses, draped tables and floral china – you will not be disappointed by the bedrooms. Each one is individually decorated, and all are delightful: sophisticated and very feminine in English style, full of thoughtful touches. Three rooms have private balconies, at no extra cost. Best of all is the villa with its pillared portico, carved flourishes on its four façades and sweeping staircase. The hotel now has its own restaurant, beautifully decorated with stone walls and pillars and an enchanting mural depicting the highlights of the region as seen from a balcony.

The owners have prepared a helpful list of local information, including routes you can follow on the hotel's bicycles. There are two good restaurants nearby: Da Lino in Solighetto (see page 85) and Da Gigetto in Miane (be sure to visit the wine cellars). **Nearby** 11thC abbey; Palladian villas; Asolo (20 km).

Via Martiri della Libertà, 31051 Follina, Treviso
Tel 0438 971277
Fax 0438 970001
E-mail info@hotelabbazia.it
Website www.hotelabbazia.it
Location in town centre, facing the abbey; parking
Meals breakfast, dinner
Prices LL
Rooms 24; 16 double and twin, one single, 7 suites, all with shower, bath or jacuzzi bath; all rooms have phone, TV, hairdrier; 12 have air-conditioning and safe
Facilities breakfast room, terrace, sitting room, tea room, garden
Credit cards AE, DC, MC, V
Disabled not suitable
Pets not accepted
Closed never
Proprietors Giovanni and Ivana Zanon

Veneto

Country villa apartments, Gargagnago

Foresteria Serègo Alighieri

In 1353, the son of Dante, who had been exiled in Verona, bought Casal dei Ronchi, and there his direct descendants have lived ever since. Today, overseen by Count Pieralvise Serègo Alighieri, the estate is a prosperous producer of Valpolicella wines (much improved in recent years and shaking off their 'cheap and nasty' reputation) as well as olive oil, balsamic vinegar, honey, jams and rice. The family home is a lovely yellow ochre building fronted by formal gardens which overlook the vineyards. Beyond are the former stables, now beautifully converted to make eight apartments, simple yet sophisticated, sleeping two to four people. In each one you find a gleaming chrome kitchen, country furniture, soothing green cotton fabrics, white walls, marble bathrooms. No. 8 spirals up a slim tower: minute sitting room, stairs to a minute kitchen, more stairs to the bedroom. Open a door in the bedhead and there's a tiny window behind. No. 1 is the most spacious, with dining table and elegant chairs. Breakfast is served in a room decorated with old family photographs on the ground floor. Dinner can be arranged for eight people or more. There are some good restaurants nearby. **Nearby** Verona (18 km); Lake Garda (14 km).

37020 Gargagnago di
Valpolicella, Verona
Tel 045 7703622
Fax 045 7703523
E-mail serego@easynet.it
Website www.seregoalighieri.it
Location signposted off the
road from Pedemonte to San
Ambrogio, 18 km NE of
Verona; in own extensive
grounds with ample parking
Meals breakfast
Prices apartment sleeping 2–4
people LL per night; weekly

rates available
Rooms 8 apartments for 2, 3 or
4 people, each with kitchen,
bathroom with shower, phone,
TV, air-conditioning
Facilities reception, breakfast
room, terrace, meeting room,
estate produce shop
Credit cards AE, MC, V
Disabled not suitable
Pets accepted
Closed Jan
Proprietor Conte Pieralvise
Serègo Alighieri

Veneto

Town guest-house, Lazise

Alla Grotta

The pretty and colourful little fishing port of Lazise (with a busy Tuesday market) is an ideal base for exploring Lake Garda and Verona, which is close by. Less popular than Sirmione, it is noted for the quality of its fish restaurants, one of which is Alla Grotta, an ochre red building in a delightful location overlooking the little harbour, always full of congenial activity and from which you can take trips on the lake

In the smart, spacious dining room, with rustic stone walls and a *forno al legno* in the centre for grilling fresh fish, we enjoyed a delicious lunch of grilled sardines and sea bass, served with excellent mixed salads. The restaurant is the *raison d'être* of family-owned and run Alla Grotta, but upstairs are also 14 neat, well-turned-out bedrooms, which are in heavy demand during high season (book well in advance). Though they could not be described as characterful, and don't pretend to be other than standard hotel bedrooms, they are of a fair size and decorated with a bit of colour and imagination, and the odd piece of country furniture. The two suites have lake views. There is no sitting room for residents. New to the guide: readers' reports welcome.
Nearby Sirmione; Pescheria; Verona.

Via Fontana 8, 37017 Lazise, Verona
Tel 045 7580035
Fax 045 7580035
Location in the town centre, overlooking the harbour
Meals breakfast, lunch, dinner
Prices L
Rooms 14; 12 double, 2 suites, all with shower or bath; all rooms have phone, TV
Facilities dining room, terrace, bar
Credit cards MC, V

Disabled access difficult
Pets not accepted
Closed mid-Dec to mid-Feb; restaurant closed Tue
Proprietor Barato family

Veneto

Agriturismo, Levada

Gargan

The setting is rural, on a working farm, and the farmhouse is typical – attractive enough, but not especially prepossessing. A donkey brays in the garden. We walked in quite unprepared for the level of sophistication of this *agriturismo*; it's in a league of its own. The ground floor comprises a hallway with cool white walls and beams painted pale green, plus five interconnecting dining rooms. Furnished only with antiques, these rooms have delicate lace curtains, timbered ceilings, and an array of pictures on their white walls. Our visit coincided with Sunday lunch, and every table was immaculately laid with a white cloth, fine china and gleaming silver; an open fire crackled in the hearth.

The ingredients used in the cooking are mainly produced on the farm. Signora Calzavara is in charge of the cooking and provides a full American breakfast and other meals when required.

The six bedrooms are enchanting. Floors are strewn with rugs; most have wrought-iron bedheads and fine walnut furniture. It's best to book by fax unless you speak Italian.

Nearby Palladian villas; Venice (20 km); Padua (26 km).

Via Marco Polo 2, Levada di Piombino Dese, Padova
Tel 049 9350308
Fax 049 9350016
E-mail agargan@tin.it
Website www.gargan.it
Location 20 km N of Venice, in Levada take Via G. Carducci opposite the church and turn left into Via Marco Polo; in own garden with ample parking
Meals breakfast, lunch, dinner
Prices L
Rooms 6; 4 double and twin, 2 family rooms, all with shower; all rooms have TV
Facilities dining rooms, sitting area, garden
Credit cards not accepted
Disabled access difficult
Pets not accepted
Closed Jan, Aug
Proprietors Calzavara family

Veneto

Country villa, Mira Porte

Villa Margherita

Another country villa in the Venetian hinterland, this time on the Brenta Riviera, overlooking a flat, industrial landscape but offering peace, seclusion and acres of real estate for your money, while being well placed for excursions into Venice, which is just ten kilometres away.

Villa Margherita was built in the 17thC as a nobleman's country retreat, and has been open as a hotel since 1987. It is less imposing outside than some of its rival villa-hotels, but attractively furnished within, particularly in the public areas. The yellow and blue breakfast room is gloriously light, with French windows on to the garden, while the sitting room has murals (the principal one portrays a bevy of naked nymphs cavorting on the banks of the Brenta), an open fireplace and some beautiful lamps, vases and antique clocks. Bedrooms, refurbished recently, are thoroughly comfortable; the best lead to the breakfast terrace.

The Dal Corso family is the driving force behind the hotel and its highly regarded restaurant, 200 metres away across a terrifying road. A lively place, buzzing with locals as well as hotel guests, it specializes in mouthwatering seafood.

Nearby Venice (10 km); Padua (20 km).

Via Nazionale 416, 30030 Mira, Venezia
Tel 041 4265800
Fax 041 4265838
E-mail hvillam@tin.it
Website www.romantikhotels.com/rhmira
Location on banks of Brenta river at Mira Porte at the E end of Mira, 10 km W of Venice; in own grounds with ample parking
Meals breakfast, lunch, dinner
Prices LL

Rooms 19; 18 double and twin, 3 with bath, 15 with shower; 1 single with shower; all rooms have phone, TV, air-conditioning, minibar, hairdrier
Facilities breakfast room, sitting room, bar, restaurant (200 m walk), garden, jogging track
Credit cards AE, DC, MC, V
Disabled several rooms on ground floor **Pets** accepted
Closed never
Proprietors Dal Corso family

Veneto

Agriturismo, Modolo

Fulcio Miari Fulcis

The *raison d'être* of the little hamlet of Modolo is the beautiful 16thC Villa Miari, quite a surprising find in this rural backwater. Nearby is the home of Fulcio Miari Fulcis, nephew of the present owner of Villa Miari, his charming Milanese wife and their young children. And this is very much a *home;* in winter wood is piled up outside, in summer brightly coloured bedclothes hang out of the window to air; children and family pets potter about. There is a pinball machine and a barbecue area. Fulcio is a ski instructor at nearby Nevegàl and also keeps horses, organizing riding expeditions for his guests.

The handsome, green-shuttered farmhouse is typical of the area with the main two-storey building abutting a broad three-storey tower: this wing is reserved for guests. Bedrooms are homely and charming, with a profusion of armchairs and ottomans and an assortment of gaily patterned fabrics. You have a one-in-six chance of occupying a huge hand-carved four-poster from Thailand. Large wood-framed windows give views of the rising hills, and there are rustic beamed ceilings, wooden floors and old doors.

Nearby Belluno (7 km); Nevegàl ski area (10 km).

Località Modolo, 32124
Castion, Belluno
Tel/Fax 0437 927198
Location from Belluno, follow signs for Nevegàl; after Castion, turn left signposted Modolo; the house is on the right
Meals breakfast
Prices L
Rooms 6; 4 double and twin, 2 family; 3 communal bathrooms
Facilities breakfast room, sitting room, sauna, barbecue, garden, horse-riding

Credit cards not accepted
Children welcome
Disabled not suitable
Pets accepted
Closed never
Proprietor Fulcio Miari Fulcis

Veneto

Country villa, Ospedaletto di Pescantina

Villa Quaranta

Ospedaletto earned its name as a stopping-off point on the way to and from the Brenner pass; the 13thC Chapel of Santa Maria di Mezza Campagna, with its Ligozzi frescoes, was where travellers put up. This now forms one side of the Villa Quaranta's pretty inner courtyard: the remainder of the buildings are 17thC. Yet though the hotel's setting, in lovely grounds, is impressive, and its main building imposing, the atmosphere is one of quiet informality. In the restaurant, for example, you are confronted by a vast stone staircase, awe-inspiring frescoed walls, stone-arched doors and tiled floors; yet the ambience is relaxed and the food good value.

Since we last wrote about the hotel for our all-Italy guide, considerable changes have taken place. Bedrooms have proliferated; new ones are spacious, if uniform, with luxury bathrooms, tasteful reproduction furniture, brass fittings, deep-pile carpets. There's a piano bar, pool, terrace bar ... and across the park a luxurious beauty and fitness centre ... and a disco. This last caused a blot on our otherwise happy stay as the roar of revellers' engines continued into the small hours.

Nearby Verona (minibus to opera); Lake Garda (12 km).

Via Brennero, 37026 Ospedaletto di Pescantina, Verona
Tel 045 6767300
Fax 045 6767301
Location on SS12, 15 km NW of Verona, in own park with ample parking
Meals breakfast, lunch, dinner
Prices LL
Rooms 70; 59 single, double and twin, 11 suites, all with bath; all rooms have phone, TV, air-conditioning, minibar, hairdrier
Facilities sitting room, dining rooms, bar, TV room, swimming pool, 2 tennis courts (1 indoor), fitness/beauty centre, meeting centre, park with lake
Credit cards AE, DC, MC, V
Disabled access possible
Pets not accepted
Closed hotel never; restaurant Mon
Manager Persio Munoz

Veneto

Country villa, Pedemonte

Villa del Quar

Situated in the fertile Valpolicella valley, this 'typical patrician dwelling' has for the past six years been a luxury hotel, a member of Relais et Châteaux. The ebullient owner and her family live in the fine main villa, while her hotel occupies the east wing. Public rooms in particular make a great impression. The galleried sitting room, an enclosed arcade with beamed roof, is delightfully light, airy and sophisticated. The two dining rooms – resplendent with mirrors, Venetian torches, vast Murano glass chandelier, cream silk tablecloths and elegant dining chairs – are also extremely attractive and make delightful rooms in which to eat. Bedrooms are more restrained, masculine even, many with lovely old cupboard doors. Bathrooms feel luxurious, swathed in prettily coloured marble. If you take a suite, ask for the one with its own terrace, which is no more expensive.

In summer a white awning covers the terrace and the immaculate pool sparkles invitingly. The villa's setting, though quiet, is not so idyllic; though it is surrounded by a sea of vines, the road is close by and there is a modern housing development on the nearest hillside.

Nearby Verona (11 km); Lake Garda (20 km).

Via Quar 12,
37020 Pedemonte, Verona
Tel 045 6800681
Fax 045 6800604
E-mail villadelquar@c-point.it
Website
www.integra.Fr/relaischateaux/delquar
Location in Pedemonte follow signs for Verona and hotel at traffic lights; after about 1,500 m turn right for hotel; in own grounds with ample parking **Meals** breakfast, lunch, dinner **Prices** LLL

Rooms 22; 19 double and twin, 3 suites, all with bath; all rooms have phone, TV, air-conditioning, minibar, hairdrier, safe **Facilities** sitting room, 2 dining rooms, breakfast room, bar, terrace, swimming pool, small gym, meeting room **Credit cards** AE, DC, MC, V **Disabled** rooms on ground floor **Pets** accepted **Closed** 15th Nov to 15th Mar **Proprietors** Evelina Acampora and Leopoldo Montresor

Veneto

Restaurant-with-rooms, Pieve d'Alpago

Dolada

A twisting road leads from the Alpago valley to Pieve, and then corkscrews on up to the little hamlet of Plois. Dolada turns out to be a handsome turn-of-the-century building with faded apricot walls and green-shuttered windows with a little garden which looks out over snow-capped mountains and the Santa Croce lake and valley far below. Our inspector reports that although the food was well worth the trip from Belluno, he was glad to be staying the night and not negotiating the hairpin bends after dinner 'although the bright pink of our modern bedroom was a bit of a shocker after our delicious meal in the more sophisticated and mellow surroundings of the dining room'. Each room is themed in a different colour, which can cause a mild feeling of panic if the colour grates.

   The point of Dolada is its restaurant, Michelin-starred, which deftly mixes traditional Italian dishes with inventive new ones, and offers a very good wine list. In a series of rooms, lace-clothed tables are set with silver cutlery, with ribbed aluminium lamps suspended over each. Chef Enzo De Pra and his wife, Rossanna, are very friendly.

Nearby Belluno (20 km); Nevegàl ski area (18 km).

Via Dolada 21, 32010 Plois in
Pieve d'Alpago, Belluno
Tel 0437 479141
Fax 0437 478068
E-mail dolade@tin.it
Website www.dolade.it
Location in the hamlet of Plois,
signposted from Pieve
d'Alpago; ample parking
Meals breakfast, lunch, dinner
Prices L
Rooms 7 double and twin, all
with shower; all rooms have
phone, TV

Facilities dining room, terrace,
garden
Credit cards AE, DC, MC, V
Disabled access difficult to
bedrooms
Pets accepted
Closed Jan to Feb; restaurant
closed Mon and Tues lunch
except July and Aug
Proprietors Enzo and Rossanna
De Pra

Veneto

Country villa, Portobuffolé

Villa Giustinian

A solid rectangular white pile with two chimneys stuck incongruously on top like candles on a birthday cake, this villa is surrounded by a park of green lawns filled with statues and enclosed by a high hedge, which cuts it off from the outside world. Rooms are of awesome dimensions: hardly intimate, but certainly impressive. There are several public rooms in pale pastels with newly restored plaster moulding and frescoes, but nowhere cosy to sit; nevertheless, the atmosphere is pleasantly unstuffy. A balustraded stairway leads to an immense gallery, frescoed from floor to ceiling.

There are eight suites in the main villa, usually used for business purposes (several have their own meeting rooms). Two have extremely elaborate original plasterwork: in one the bed is enveloped in an over-the-top canopy of draped figures, cherubs and garlands. Easier to live with are the simpler rooms in the old stable block, with beams, pretty fabrics and decent reproduction furniture. In the same block are the restaurant, a stylish setting for excellent fish, and the *enoteca*, where you can sample a fine collection of wines and eat a snack.

Nearby Pordenone (15 km); Treviso (37 km); Venice (55 km).

Via Giustiniani 11, 31019
Portobuffolé, Treviso
Tel 0422 850244
Fax 0422 850260
Location 9 km N of Oderzo, in
own grounds with ample
parking
Meals breakfast, lunch, dinner
Prices L
Rooms 43; 28 double and twin,
1 with bath, 27 with shower; 7
single with shower; 8 suites with
bath or shower; all rooms have
phone, TV, fax/modem (on
request), air-conditioning,
minibar, hairdrier, safe
Facilities breakfast/sitting and
conference rooms, bar,
restaurant, *enoteca*, terrace,
garden
Credit cards AE, DC, MC, V
Disabled no special facilities
Pets not accepted
Closed 2-3 weeks in Aug
Proprietors Berto family

Veneto

Country hotel, San Bonifacio

Relais Villabella

Don't be put off by the hideous sign set into the portico which spoils an otherwise handsome terracotta frontage. Inside, the Relais Villabella lives up to its name. Built as a humble rice mill and retaining its stone floors and timbered ceilings, it has been cleverly converted to a sophisticated hotel with numerous elegant public rooms and just nine equally elegant bedrooms. Two dining rooms testify to the importance placed on food. The smaller is a refined room, furnished in green, with an open hearth and intimate atmosphere, often used for private dinners. The more formal main restaurant has floor-to-ceiling windows looking on to the garden. The emphasis of the excellent menu is on regional dishes – pasta, risotto, polenta. In a very different style, the piano bar has clusters of shiny black cane tables and chairs around a dance floor, where convention delegates and divas from the Verona opera may smooch the night away.

Bedrooms lead off mysterious, dimly-lit corridors, which might be romantic if you weren't in constant danger of tripping. Some rooms shimmer with mirrored walls and metres of gold and green shot silk fabric; all have luxurious marble bathrooms.
Nearby Vicenza (30 km); Verona (20 km); Palladian villas.

Località Villabella, 37047 San Bonifacio, Verona
Tel 045 6101777
Fax 045 6101799
Location take Castello exit from Soave motorway or sign for Cavalca from SS11, after Sotto Portico, hotel is on the left
Meals breakfast, lunch, dinner
Prices L
Rooms 9 double and twin, all with bath; all rooms have phone, TV, air-conditioning, minibar, hairdrier

Facilities sitting area, dining rooms, piano bar, meeting room, garden
Credit cards AE, MC, V
Disabled not suitable
Pets accepted
Closed restaurant Sun, Mon; piano bar Mon
Proprietor Mario Cherubin

Veneto

Lakeside hotel, San Vigilio

Locanda San Vigilio

In general the east side of Lake Garda is less upmarket than the west but this hotel's idyllic setting, on a lush peninsula dotted with olive trees and cypresses, is a conspicuous exception. The property is owned by Conte Agostino Guarienti, who lives in the 16thC villa that dominates the headland. An air of discreet exclusivity pervades the *locanda* (royalty are among regular guests) yet the atmosphere is far from stuffy. Of the public rooms, our favourite is the elegant dining room, right on the lake, with a comfortingly creaky wooden floor. A ceramic stove occupies one corner and sideboards display plates and bottles. You can eat in here, on a little arched veranda or under huge white umbrellas on the terrace where terracotta pots overflow with flowers. Next door is a cosy sitting room.

The seven bedrooms in the main house are all different, though they have beautiful antiques and fabrics in common. Only one has no view. Other bedrooms are in separate buildings and more rustic in style. In the evening the place comes into its own: with the day trippers gone, guests can wander the peninsula or sit with a drink at one of the Taverna's vine-shaded tables.
Nearby Garda (2 km); Verona (45 km); ferry services (4 km).

San Vigilio, 37016 Garda, Verona
Tel 045 7256688
Fax 045 7256551
E-mail sanvigilio@gardanews.it
Website www.gardanews.it/sanvigilio
Location 2 km W of Garda, on promontory; parking available 150 m away
Meals breakfast, lunch, dinner
Prices LL-LLLL
Rooms 14; 11 double and twin, 3 suites, all with bath or shower; all rooms have phone, TV, air-conditioning, minibar, hairdrier; most rooms have safe
Facilities sitting room, dining room, bar, terrace, walled garden
Credit cards AE, DC, MC, V
Disabled not suitable
Pets accepted
Closed Nov to just before Easter
Proprietor Conte Agostino Guarienti

Veneto

Town villa, Scorzè

Villa Soranzo Conestabile

Standing at the centre of the hard-working town of Scorzè, this aristocratic villa dates back to the 16thC, but was remodelled in the 18thC in elegant neoclassical style. Visible from its earliest period (especially if you take room No. 1) are fragments of gorgeous School of Veronese frescoes. There are also fine ceilings and floors, an impressive double staircase and a park modelled in the early 19thC in Romantic English style. The spacious first-floor rooms are somewhat staid but full of character, recalling the last century when they were the bedrooms of the noble Conestabile family, retaining their lofty proportions, and, in some cases, original faux marble walls. Rooms on the second floor, formerly the household quarters, are plainer but spacious and furnished in different styles.

On her March visit our inspector reports that she ate alone in the dining room, but was comforted by the familial ambience, with copper pans hanging from the ceiling and old dressers laden with wine bottles, and by a simple but well-prepared set menu. She also notes that her visit was marred by one of the coolest welcomes in reception that she can remember.

Nearby Riviera del Brenta; Venice (24 km); Padua (30 km).

Via Roma 1, 30037 Scorzè, Venezia
Tel 041 445027
Fax 041 5840088
E-mail vsoranzo@tin.it
Location in Scorzè, 24 km NW of Venice, in own grounds with ample parking
Meals breakfast, lunch, dinner
Prices L
Rooms 20; 14 double and twin, 3 single, all with bath or shower; 3 suites; all rooms have phone, TV

Facilities sitting room, dining room, bar, breakfast room, meeting room, terrace, garden
Credit cards AE, DC, MC, V
Disabled not suitable
Pets accepted
Closed restaurant only, Nov to Mar
Proprietors Martinelli family

Veneto

Locanda da Lino

The creation of an inspired chef, Lino Toffolin, this restaurant became an institution. Championed by the diva Toti Dal Monte, the young Lino was soon cooking for the *glitterati* and being patronized by stars such as Marcello Mastrioni. Now run by Lino's family, the restaurant seems to have lost some of its verve in recent years. One long room, with smaller rooms leading off it, can seat 400 for dinner at full stretch. The ceilings are hung idiosyncratically with hundreds of copper pots. A table in the 'inner sanctum' enables you to glimpse food being grilled over a blazing furnace. From a menu of local delicacies, we particularly enjoyed *antipasto misto della Locanda, braciole di vitello ai ferri* and *polpettine in umido con polenta*, and there's an impressive wine list from the beautifully laid-out cellar.

The bedrooms are in annexes and range from comfortable doubles to the extravagantly rococo Elsa Vazzoler suite with its bright blue walls, enormous gilt lamps, and cherubs above the bed. The L-shaped entrance/bar/breakfast area is also furnished with rococo pieces, mixed eclectically but successfully with modern art. More reports please.

Nearby Palladian villas; Asolo (20 km).

Via Brandolini 31, 31050
Solighetto, Treviso
Tel 0438 82150/842377
Fax 0438 980577
E-mail dalino@trun.it
Website www.seven.it/locanda-da-lino
Location in Solighetto on the Follina road; with ample parking
Meals breakfast, lunch, dinner
Prices L
Rooms 17; 10 double and twin, 7 suites, all with bath; all rooms have phone, TV, minibar,
hairdrier
Facilities breakfast area/bar, restaurant, terrace
Credit cards AE, DC, MC, V
Disabled several rooms on ground floor
Pets accepted
Closed restaurant Mon, Christmas Day, July
Proprietors 'Lino' family

Veneto

Lakeside hotel, Torri del Benaco

Gardesana

Torri del Benaco is one of the showpiece fishing villages which are dotted along the shore of Lake Garda, and Gardesana is in a plum position. It is a treat to tuck into the chef's speciality fish soup on the delightful first-floor dining terrace which overlooks the central *piazza*, 14thC castle and bustling port. The wrought-iron balustrade is decked with cascading geraniums, the tables are elegant, the waiters smartly uniformed, and the food, particularly the fish, fresh and delicious. It makes a perfect vantage point for watching the boats come and go, and the changing colours of the lake. Drinks can also be taken on the ground-floor terrace, which extends out on to the *piazza*.

The building has a long history, as its exterior would suggest, with its stone arches and mellow stucco walls; but the entire interior has been smartly modernized in recent years to produce an essentially modern and very comfortable hotel. The green and white bedrooms are almost all identical: wooden furnishings, soft fabrics, plenty of little extras. If you can, try to book one of the corner rooms; these have the advantage of facing both the lake and the *piazza*.

Nearby Bardolino (11 km); Malcesine (21 km); Gardaland.

Piazza Calderini 20, 37010
Torri del Benaco, Verona
Tel 045 7225411
Fax 045 7225771
E-mail gardesana@easynet.it
Website www.hotel-gardesana.com
Location in town centre, on waterfront, in pedestrian zone; unload at hotel, private parking 150 m away
Meals breakfast, dinner
Prices L
Rooms 34; 31 double, 3 single, all with shower; all rooms have

phone, TV, air-conditioning
(Jul and Aug)
Facilities dining room, bar, lift, terrace
Credit cards AE, DC, MC, V
Disabled no special facilities
Pets not accepted
Closed Nov and Dec
Proprietor Giuseppe Lorenzini

Veneto

Restaurant-with-rooms, Trissino

Relais Ca' Masieri

The countryside around industrial Arzignano is uninspiring, but things improve as you wind your way to Masieri through willow-fringed meadows. Through wrought-iron gates and at the end of a long drive, the sight of Ca' Masieri itself, a fine old shuttered mansion with swimming pool and shady terrace further lifts the spirits. In our case, they were immediately cast down, because we were late and the chef had just gone home: we had been dreaming of the much-vaunted food all morning. The sight of the charming little restaurant, its walls decorated with delicate 18thC frescoes, only made our disappointment worse. Had we been in time, we might have had the salad of crayfish tails followed by risotto with herbs, and then the casserole of pigeon ...

The bedrooms are in an adjacent building which retains its old wooden beamed ceilings, but is otherwise furnished in contemporary style. Two rooms have spiral metal staircases from a sitting area up to the mezzanine beds. No. 201 is huge, with a terrace overlooking the hills and Trissino. There are pretty bedspreads in William Morris leaf-print, curvy modern tables, and stylish bathrooms with walls painted the colour of aluminium.
Nearby Vicenza (21 km); Verona (49 km).

Località Masieri, Via Masieri, 36070 Trissino, Vicenza
Tel 0445 490122
Fax 0445 490455
Location from Trissino, follow signs to Masieri, and in Via Masieri to Ca' Masieri up a private drive; ample parking
Meals breakfast, lunch, dinner
Prices L
Rooms 12; 5 double, 2 single, 5 apartments, all with shower; all rooms have phone, TV, minibar; 9 have air-conditioning
Facilities sitting room, bar, breakfast room, dining room, terrace, swimming pool
Credit cards AE, MC, V
Disabled not suitable
Pets accepted
Closed late Jan to mid-Feb
Proprietor Angelo Vassena

Veneto

Town hotel, Verona

Colomba d'Oro

The hotel stands opposite the friendly little Torcolo (see page 103) which, though simple, is much more in the spirit of our guide. Nevertheless, the smart, slick Colomba d'Oro should not be ignored, if for no other reason than its eye-catching lobby, muralled with consummate skill by a young artist in 1996. Three months and two assistants later, the result was a charming evocation of Renaissance Verona, with faux marble pillars and statues, balcony scenes on the ceiling and dreamy vistas of lakes, rivers and Roman ruins on the walls.

A hotel since 1880, the Tapparini family have been in charge since 1927 and have engaged in constant refurbishment over the years. Today, it is in excellent condition; bedrooms are *à la mode,* some with water-silk fabric on the walls and matching bedspreads, others in glossy modern style, with gleaming *spatolato* walls in golden yellow, pale green or deep pink, and polished wood fittings. Despite the romantic foyer, a fairly impersonal, business-oriented air pervades, especially in the breakfast room and the large sitting room, with its abundance of formal leather seating.

Nearby Arena; Via Mazzini, Piazza delle Erbe.

Via Cattaneo 10, 37121 Verona
Tel 045 595300
Fax 045 594974
Location in city centre, just off Piazza Brà; parking in hotel garage or public car park in Piazza Cittadella
Meals LL
Rooms 51; 26 double and twin, 15 single, 10 junior suites; 39 rooms with bath, 12 with shower; all rooms have phone, TV, air-conditioning, minibar, hairdrier

Facilities sitting room, breakfast room, bar, meeting room, lift
Credit cards AE, DC, MC, V
Disabled access difficult
Pets accepted
Closed never
Proprietor Alberto Tapparini

Veneto

Town hotel, Verona

Gabbia d'Oro

This stylish hotel in a 17thC *palazzo*, luxurious but never ostentatious, boasts an attention to detail rarely encountered nowadays. A small, beautifully wrapped gift awaits your arrival, and the staff are as charming and polished as the hotel itself. The public rooms, entered through massive wood doors with gilt decoration, are comfortable as well as elegant: there are plenty of places in which to sit and relax, and sofas are large and deep. Wooden floors, beams and brickwork are much in evidence; the sitting room shares one wall with the Gardello Tower. Furnishings, chandeliers, silver-framed photographs, ornaments and antiques are always in keeping. Little lamps lend a glow to the panelled bar, and the new orangery is restful, with its green and white colour scheme and view to the terrace.

Frescoes, restored or reproduced from the originals, recur as friezes both downstairs and in the bedrooms. Suites outnumber doubles. In almost all, beds are shrouded in a canopy of antique lace. No. 404, dark red with sloping walls, rafters, and nooks and crannies, is so romantic that it's normally chosen for honeymooners. Prices are high, but we felt justifiably so.

Nearby Piazza delle Erbe; Loggia del Consiglio; Arena.

Corso Portoni Borsari 4a, 37121 Verona
Tel 045 8003060
Fax 045 590293
E-mail gabbiadoro@easynet.it
Website www.gardalake.it
Location in medieval centre of the city, S of Porta Borsari; garage parking available
Meals breakfast
Prices LLL-LLLL
Rooms 27; 8 double and twin, 19 suites, all with bath or shower; all rooms have phone, TV, air-conditioning, minibar, hairdrier, safe
Facilities breakfast room, sitting room, orangery, bar, meeting room, lift, terrace
Credit cards AE, DC, MC, V
Disabled access difficult
Pets accepted
Closed never
Proprietor Signora Balzarro

Veneto

Town hotel, Verona

Torcolo

The Torcolo is an inexpensive hotel in an excellent location at the heart of lively Verona. 'Its most outstanding quality,' writes one recent guest, 'was the warmth and friendliness of our welcome and the consistent helpfulness of the staff'. Every room is individually decorated in varying styles – Italian 18thC, art nouveau, modern – and all are fresher and have more charm than one normally finds at this price. Ours contained a complete set of Liberty-style bedroom furniture which had belonged to owner Silvia Pommari's parents when they first married. It was set off by white linen curtains and a colourful patchwork bedspread. Ceramic tiled bathrooms are somewhat cramped; the best have separate shower cubicles. Rooms are double-glazed against the considerable street sounds (people, not cars) but, despite air-conditioning, they can get fuggy, especially in warm weather. Breakfast, including a jug of fresh orange juice, a good assortment of bread and croissants and yoghurt, can be taken in your room, which might be preferable to the rather cramped little breakfast room. In summer, it is served buffet-style in the small off-street courtyard.

Nearby Arena; Via Mazzini, Piazza delle Erbe.

Vicolo Listone 3, 37121 Verona
Tel 045 8007512
Fax 045 8004058
Location just off Piazza Brà; park in public car park in Piazza Cittadella
Meals breakfast
Prices L
Rooms 17 double, twin and single, 2 family, one with bath and 18 with shower; all rooms have phone, TV, air-conditioning, hairdrier; 10 rooms have minibar and safe

Facilities sitting area, breakfast room, courtyard, lift
Credit cards AE, MC, V
Closed 10–31 Jan
Disabled access difficult
Pets accepted
Proprietors Silvia Pommari and Diana Castellani

Veneto

Country villa, Zerman di Mogliano Veneto

Villa Condulmer

For the price of a three star in San Marco you can stay in this impressive 18thC villa a 20-minute drive away. Flanked by low annexes, it stands four-square in a miniature park landscaped by Sebatoni. From the moment we walked in we were struck by the sheer scale not only of the rooms, but the furnishings. The vast central hall is decorated with baroque stucco in different hues, inset with murals. Two extravagantly large Murano chandeliers hang from the high ceiling, but armchairs make it a room to sit in, not just admire. A pair of grand pianos bear witness to Verdi's visits here. The more dilapidated is his; the other, a copy. The menu in the restful pale green and white dining room verges on the pretentious, but don't pass up the chance of a drink in the intimate stuccoed bar.

The most exotic – and expensive – bedrooms are the upstairs suites (Ronald Reagan slept in No. 4). The double rooms in the main villa have been redecorated using bright silk damasks, but we preferred the more restrained annexe rooms, where the peace and quiet, the comfortable beds and the heavenly linen sheets should guarantee a good night's sleep.
Nearby Palladian villas; Venice (18 km).

Via Zermanese 1, 31020
Zerman di Mogliano Veneto,
Treviso
Tel 041 457100
Fax 041 457134
E-mail condulme@tin.it
Location 12 km S of Treviso, N
of road to Mogliano Veneto; in
own grounds with ample
parking
Meals breakfast, lunch, dinner
Prices LL
Rooms 43 double and twin,
single, junior suites, 8

apartments, all with bath or
shower; all rooms have phone,
TV, air-conditioning, minibar,
hairdrier
Facilities breakfast room, bar,
sitting rooms, meeting room,
TV room, dining rooms,
garden, swimming pool, tennis
courts, golf (9,18 hole)
Credit cards AE, DC, MC, V
Disabled access difficult
Pets accepted
Closed never
Proprietor Davide Zuin

Lombardia

Lakeside restaurant-with-rooms, Gardone Riviera

Villa Fiordaliso

Michelin-starred Villa Fiordaliso has been well-known as one of the best restaurants in Northern Italy for some years, but it is also a chic and romantic small hotel. Built in 1902, the pale pink and white lakeside villa was home to Gabriele d'Annunzio, and later to Claretta Petacci, Mussolini's mistress. Inside, the intricately carved wood and marble work on walls, floors and doorways and the splendid gold and frescoed ceilings are the perfectly preserved remnants of another age. A magnificent Venetian-style marble staircase, with columns and delicate wrought ironwork leads from the reception hall at garden level to the intimate first-floor restaurant and up to the seven luxurious bedrooms. Three of these have been left with their original furniture and decoration. The Claretta suite, a room of impressive dimensions with terrace and lake view, has a stunning marble bathroom. Other rooms are lighter in style with fresh wallpapers and fabrics.

The shady garden, bordering the lake (and, unfortunately, the main road), is a wonderful setting for the elegant summer restaurant, immaculately decked out in a terracotta and white colour scheme.

Nearby Brescia (40 km); Sirmione (35 km).

Corso Zanardelli 132, 25083
Gardone Riviera, Brescia
Tel 0365 20158
Fax 0365 290011
E-mail fiordaliso@relaischateaux.fr
Location on SS572, 3 km NE of Salò; in grounds with ample parking
Meals breakfast, lunch, dinner
Prices LL-LLL
Rooms 7; 5 double, 2 suites, all with bath or shower; all rooms have phone, TV, air-conditioning, minibar

Facilities dining room, sitting room, tower with bar, terraces, garden
Credit cards AE, DC, MC, V
Disabled access to restaurant possible
Pets not accepted
Closed Jan to mid-Mar; restaurant Mon, Tues lunch
Proprietors Tosetti family

Lombardia

Lakeside villa, Gardone Riviera

Villa del Sogno

Built in 1904 as the holiday home of an Austrian silk industrialist, this imposing villa became a hotel in 1938. Like so many of the hotels around Lake Garda, it has an amazing position, above the lake but near enough to feel part of the lakeside scene. It is approached by a long winding drive and cradled in exotic gardens, where we stumbled upon two little neoclassical temples. An extension added in the 1980s contains some rather ordinary rooms, including the reception (disappointing when you first arrive). But go through to the wood-panelled hall and staircase and you'll find much more character. The huge wooden fireplace and painted ceramic tiles reveal the villa's Austrian heritage, which is only slightly at odds with the stone arches, Grecian urns, and other neoclassical flourishes.

Armchairs in cheerful floral prints and a bar at one end make the sitting room especially congenial. There is also a refined restaurant in two rooms, where the parquet floor gleams almost as much as the silver candlesticks. Upstairs, there are several enormous suites, furnished traditionally. Rooms in the new wing are lighter with their own terraces.

Nearby beach (300 m); Brescia (50 km).

Via Zanardelli 107, 25083
Gardone Riviera, Brescia
Tel 0365 290181
Fax 0365 290230
E-mail villadelsogno@gardalake.it
Website www.gardalake.it/villadelsogno
Location 2 km N of Gardone,
off the SS45; in own grounds
with ample parking
Meals breakfast, lunch, dinner
Prices LLL
Rooms 32; 25 double and twin,
20 with bath, 5 with shower; 7
suites with bath; all rooms have

phone, TV, hairdrier; 9 have
air-conditioning
Facilities sitting room/bar,
dining room, sauna, solarium,
lift, terrace, garden, swimming
pool, tennis courts
Credit cards AE, DC, MC, V
Disabled no special facilities
Pets accepted
Closed mid-Oct to end Mar (or
Easter if earlier)
Proprietors Caldaran family

Lombardia

Lakeside hotel, Gargnano

Baia d'Oro

Giambattista Terzi was born in one of a pair of neighbouring fishermen's cottages built on the edge of the lake in 1780, and his wife was the moving force behind turning them into a hotel in the 1960s. Since then the facilities have slowly been updated. To appreciate the fabulous setting, you should arrive by boat.

You can almost dip your hand in the lake from the romantic dining terrace, a splendid vantage point from which to watch night succeed day to the gentle lapping of the water. Boats dock at a little jetty also used by sunbathers. For cool nights, there's a pleasant dining room overlooking the terrace to the lake. Here Terzi's son Gabriele is in charge, and the fine, short menu consists of saltwater and freshwater fish, served simply.

The Terzis are gradually redecorating the bedrooms in slightly dubious shades of pink and blue, with painted wooden furniture, shiny fabrics and mirrored glass bedheads. Not to everyone's taste, but they are comfortable with sparkling new bathrooms, and the doubles all have lake views.

The cosy, low-ceilinged sitting room has an open fire, and Giambattista's paintings of the area cover the walls.

Nearby Gardone Riviera (12 km); Sirmione (48 km).

Via Gamberera 13, 25084
Gargnano, Brescia
Tel 0365 71171/72078
Fax 0365 72568
Location on edge of town, on lake; with private parking
Meals breakfast, lunch, dinner
Prices L
Rooms 13; 10 double and twin, 2 with bath, 8 with shower; 3 single with shower; 1 suite with bath; all rooms have phone, TV, minibar, hairdrier, safe
Facilities sitting room, dining

room, bar, terrace, sun deck
Credit cards not accepted
Disabled not suitable
Pets accepted
Closed mid-Nov to mid-Mar
Proprietors Terzi family

Lombardia

Lakeside villa, Gargnano

Villa Giulia

From a *pensione* with no private bathrooms, the Giulia has been upgraded over the years to a three-star hotel, with the renovation of existing rooms and the creation of new suites. Happily, however, this beautiful late-19thC Victorian villa with Gothic touches still retains the atmosphere of a family-run guest house. Rina Bombardelli has been here for almost five decades, and has gradually made the Giulia one of the most delightful places to stay on Lake Garda. It has a glorious location, with gardens of lawns, palm trees and oleanders, running down to a low wall at the water's edge. Only the pool looks a little scruffy.

The villa is painted the palest of pinks with dark brown shutters and woodwork. Inside, airy rooms lead off handsome corridors: a beautiful dining room with Murano chandeliers, gold walls and elegant seats; a civilized sitting room with Victorian armchairs; and bedrooms in a variety of styles: some are light and modern, others are large, with rafters, antiques and balconies. We met one unhappy solo visitor, who claimed that the singles are not nearly as attractive as the doubles. Our favourites are the rooms in the eaves with Gothic windows.
Nearby ferry services.

Via Rimembranza 20, 25084 Gargnano, Brescia
Tel 0365 71022/71289
Fax 0365 72774
E-mail hvgiulia@gardanet.it
Website www.gardalake.it/hotel.villagiulia
Location 150 m from town centre; in own gardens with ample parking
Meals breakfast, lunch, dinner
Prices LL
Rooms 23; 16 double and twin, all with bath or shower; 6 suites with bath; all rooms have phone, central heating, TV, minibar, hairdrier, safe
Facilities sitting room, TV room, dining rooms, sauna, veranda, terrace, garden, swimming pool, beach
Credit cards AE, MC, V
Disabled 2 rooms on ground floor
Pets small dogs accepted by arrangement (charge)
Closed mid-Oct to 1 week before Easter
Proprietors Bombardelli family

Lombardia

Lakeside restaurant-with-rooms, Sirmione

Grifone

Although the Grifone is one of the cheapest and simplest hotels in this guide, it also has one of the loveliest locations, and makes a great place to stay for a night or two. Essentially it is a restaurant specializing in fish, with a mouth-watering selection of *antipasto* to start. It has an enticing tree-filled terrace overlooking both Lake Garda and the ramparts of Sirmione's castle; also a tiny sandy beach.

The entrance to the hotel is found off a narrow street just inside the city walls. A small sitting room equipped with television and cheerful bamboo furniture leads to a little patio where breakfast is served, and, if the water beckons, on to the scrap of beach. Upstairs, rooms are simple, furniture is basic, but everything is spotless. Some rooms look right over the castle walls, and the five balconies are full of flowers. Those on the top floor enjoy the best views: rooftops, mountains, and of course the lake. There is no traffic noise in this pedestrian zone, but you may be woken by church bells. The younger generation of the Marcolini family – brother and sister – who now run the Grifone are friendly and helpful.

Nearby Lake Garda; Brescia (39 km); Verona (35 km).

Vicolo Bisse (Via Bocchio) 5, 25019 Sirmione, Brescia
Tel 030 916014
Fax 030 916548
Location just inside city walls, next to castle, on lake with free parking (50 m)
Meals breakfast, lunch, dinner
Prices L
Rooms 16; 12 double, twin and triple, 4 with bath, 8 with shower; 4 single all with shower
Facilities sitting room, dining room, lift, terraces, tiny beach

Credit cards not accepted
Disabled access difficult except to restaurant
Pets not accepted
Closed Nov to Easter
Proprietors Marcolini family

Friuli-Venezia Giulia

Converted mill, Bannia di Fiume Veneto

L'Ultimo Mulino

As the name suggests, this 17thC building is one of the very last functioning mills in the area. In use until the 1970s, the three old wooden wheels are still in working condition; indeed, they are set in motion in the evenings for the benefit of guests. The lovely stone house and garden are set in gentle farmland and surrounded by three rivers; the soothing sounds of water are everywhere.

Opened as a hotel in 1994, restoration work has been carried out with great taste and flair, preserving as much as possible of the original character of the house. The long, open-plan sitting room and bar area have even incorporated the hefty innards of the mill machinery. Throughout, attractive Laura Ashley fabrics are teamed with handsome antique furniture, rustic stone and woodwork, and soft, elegant lighting. The comfortable and stylish bedrooms, while different in layout, are all along similar lines with wooden fittings and pale green and cream country fabrics. Those on the second floor have attic ceilings and some have squashy sofas. The sparkling, well-equipped bathrooms are in pale grey marble.

Nearby Pordenone (10 km); Venice (80 km); Trieste (80 km).

Via Molino 45, 33080 Bannia di Fiume Veneto, Pordenone
Tel 0434 957911
Fax 0434 958483
E-mail fllonder@tin.it
Website www.centroweb.com/hotel
Location 10 km SE of Pordenone, exit from A28 at Azzano Decimo; in own garden with parking
Meals breakfast, dinner
Prices L-LL
Rooms 8 double and twin, 4 with bath, 4 with shower; all rooms have phone, TV, air-conditioning, minibar, hairdrier
Facilities breakfast room, sitting rooms, dining rooms, bar, music/conference room, garden, terrace
Credit cards AE, DC, MC, V
Disabled no special facilities
Pets accepted
Closed 10 days Jan, Aug
Proprietors Balestrieri family

Friuli-Venezia Giulia

Country villa, Rivarotta

Villa Luppis

This rambling and mellow L-shaped building, acquired by the Luppis family in the 1800s, was once a monastery. Set in gentle countryside, there is not much sign of Spartan living today; it is now a comfortable and elegant yet relaxed hotel run by Giorgio Luppis and his wife. One side of the 'L' is a long room incorporating reception hall, sitting room and bar, bright and welcoming with low, timbered ceiling and central columns. At the front of the house is the equally long main restaurant – a dreamy room with pale pink and white table linen, period furniture, antique silver and fresh flowers. There is (rather incongruously) also a piano bar with dance floor. Long corridors, softly lit and thickly carpeted, lead to the luxurious bedrooms which are furnished with period pieces, and have superior king-size beds. Fine fabrics – Regency stripes or fresh chintzes – are co-ordinated with soft carpeting, and the suites have separate sitting areas.

The villa's extensive park with its venerable old trees and green lawns has a pleasant pool and a newly built fitness centre. A minibus service runs to and from Venice – Piazzale Roma – (only 40 minutes away) every day.

Nearby Pordenone (15 km); Treviso (35 km); Venice (50 km).

Via San Martino 34, 33087 Rivarotta, Pordenone
Tel 0434 626969
Fax 0434 626228
E-mail hotel@villaluppis.it
Website www.Villaluppis.it
Location 15 km S of Pordenone; exit A4 at Cessalto, and take road for Motta di Livenza; in extensive grounds with ample parking
Meals LL
Rooms 21; 18 double and twin, 3 suites, all with bath; all rooms have phone, TV, air-conditioning, hairdrier
Facilities sitting room, dining room, bar, meeting room, lift, terraces, gardens, swimming pool, tennis court, gym
Credit cards AE, DC, MC, V
Disabled access possible
Pets accepted
Closed never
Proprietors Giorgio and Stefania Luppis

Friuli-Venezia Giulia

Converted castle, San Floriano del Collio

Golf Hotel

Unfortunately, this is one of only a handful of hotels which we were unable to inspect personally, although it has long been included in our all-Italy guide. Judging by past reports, however, we are still happy to recommend it, but we would welcome some more recent feedback.

The hotel's name, referring to its nine-hole golf course (closed Mon; green fee L45,000), gives the impression of something modern, but it is in fact two ancient renovated houses just outside the walls of Castello Formentini, which has belonged to the Formentini family since the 16thC. The present owner, Contessa Isabella Formentini, has filled the rooms of the tiny hotel with family furniture and pictures. Each beautifully decorated and spacious bedroom is named after a prestigious wine, emphasizing the vinous interest of the Formentini family. Three of them are within the castle walls, but all guests are at liberty to use the castle grounds and its swimming pool. The family also run an excellent restaurant called Castello Formentini (closed Mon, Tues lunch). This is a charming spot, with gentle, wooded countryside spread out around the hilltop castle.

Nearby Gorizia (4 km); Trieste (47 km).

Via Oslavia 2, 34070 San Floriano del Collio, Gorizia
Tel 0481 884051
Fax 0481 884052
Location in town, just outside castle walls; private grounds; parking
Meals breakfast
Prices LL
Rooms 15; 12 double and twin, 2 single, 1 suite in tower, all with bath or shower; all rooms have TV, minibar; 12 rooms have phone; 3 rooms have no phone but air-conditioning
Facilities sitting room ,breakfast room, garden, swimming pool, tennis court, nine-hole golf course
Credit cards AE, DC, MC, V
Disabled not suitable
Pets accepted
Closed Dec to Mar
Proprietor Contessa Isabella Formentini

Friuli-Venezia Giulia

Town hotel, Trieste

Grand Hotel Duchi d'Aosta

At the point where the Latin and Balkan worlds meet, close to
Italy's borders with Slovenia, Croatia and Austria, Trieste is a
town with a fascinating history. Not only did it belong to Austria,
but was its principal port until 1918, and although its importance
has faded, it still bears the architectural legacy of its years as part
of the Hapsburg Empire. The old town boasts a clutch of gracious *palazzi*; one dating from 1873 is now home to the aptly
named Grand Hotel Duchi d'Aosta. Behind a splendid pale porticoed façade, a series of large, lavishly furnished salons and a
fleet of polite, attentive staff recall the grandeur of a bygone era.
Bedrooms share the traditional elegance of the public rooms,
but with modern amenities and bathrooms. And the restaurant,
specializing in local seafood, has an excellent reputation.

Most of the sights are within walking distance of the hotel,
conveniently located at the heart of the old town, although there
is one that must not be missed on a promontory 5 km to the
west. It is the glorious white Castello di Miramare, where the
Hapsburg Archduke Maximilian lived and which is now the setting for a *son et lumière* between June and September.

Nearby Roman theatre; cathedral; port; Castello di Miramare.

Piazza Unita d'Italia 2, 34121
Trieste
Tel 040 7600011
Fax 040 366092
Website www.info-era.com/clients/duchi
Location in the old part of town
near the fort; garage parking
Meals breakfast, lunch, dinner
Prices LL
Rooms 50; 48 double and twin,
2 suites, all with bath or shower;
all rooms have phone, TV,
air conditioning, minibar,
hairdrier

Facilities sitting rooms, restau-
rant, bar
Credit cards AE, DC, MC, V
Disabled one specially adapted
room
Pets not accepted
Closed never
Manager Hedy Benvenuti

Friuli-Venezia Giulia

Town hotel, Udine

Astoria Hotel Italia

Udine is Friuli-Venezia Giulia's capital. Though a busy centre of commerce, it does have a few buildings of interest at its historic core, and we can just about recommend this, its premier hotel, which retains a certain grandeur and sense of its past (it has been a hotel since the 1850s), despite its main funtion as a business stopover. In the dining room you will be served probably the best food in the city, by friendly, helpful waiters. The hotel's bedrooms are uniform (in pink or blue), comfortable, and mostly spacious. Best are those overlooking the piazza. While staying here, don't miss the lovely 19th century interiors of the adjacent *palazzo* – now used for exhibitions and conferences. They were designed by Japelli, famous for his Caffè Pedrocchi in Padua.

On our latest inspection trip for this guide, we made a concerted effort to find more hotels in this far north-eastern corner of Italy. One hopeful contender did elude us, Pa'Krhaizar at Sauris di Sopra: though it was late April, our road was blocked by snow and we were forced to turn back. So our best new offering in this area, sadly short of interesting places to stay, remains this town hotel in Udine.

Nearby Duomo; Piazza Matteotti; Museo Civico.

Piazza XX Settembre 24, 33100 Udine
Tel 0432 505091
Fax 0432 509070
E-mail astoria@xnet.it
Location in city centre; parking
Meals breakfast, lunch, dinner
Prices LL
Rooms 75; 39 double, 33 single, 3 suites, all with bath; all rooms have phone, TV, minibar, air-conditioning, hairdrier, safe
Facilities dining room, bar, lounge, courtyard, lift

Credit cards AE, DC, MC, V
Disabled access possible
Pets accepted
Closed never
Proprietor Signora Mocchiutti

Trentino-Alto Adige

Mountain hotel, Barbiano

Bad Dreikirchen

The name of this idyllically situated hotel derives from its vicinity to the cluster of three small churches which date back to the Middle Ages. The fact that you can only reach the hotel by four-wheel-drive taxi, makes for a perfect escape.

The large old building with its shingled roof and dark wood balconies, has wonderful views and is surrounded by meadows, woods, mountains and fresh air. There's plenty of space for guests, both inside and out, and the atmosphere is comfortably rustic with an abundance of aromatic pine panelling and carved furniture. A cosy library provides a quiet corner for reading, and simple but satisfying meals are served in the pleasant dining room or on the adjacent veranda, from which the views are superb. Bedrooms in the original part of the house are particularly charming, being entirely wood-panelled.

To sum up, the words of a guest at Bad Dreikirchen in 1908, are still appropriate: 'I stayed for some days ... the weather was continually fine, the position magnificent, and the food good.' A recent guest warmly concurs. 'I fell in love with the place. Delightfully relaxed atmosphere, charming young owners.'
Nearby Bressanone (17 km); Val Gardena (10 km).

San Giacomo 6, 39040
Barbiano, Bolzano
Tel 0471 650055
Fax 0471 650044
E-mail wodenegg.matthias@rolmail.ne
Location 21 km NE of Bolzano, exit from Brennero Autostrada at Chiusa, head S through Barbiano (6 km); hotel car park on right (call and the hotel will send a jeep to collect you from car park)
Meals breakfast, lunch, dinner
Prices half board obligatory, L

Rooms 30; 12 double and twin, 15 single, 3 family, most with shower
Facilities sitting rooms, bar, restaurant, games room, library, garden, terraces, swimming pool, table tennis, tennis court (1 km)
Credit cards MC, V
Disabled access difficult
Pets accepted
Closed Nov to mid-May
Proprietors Wodenegg family

Trentino-Alto Adige

Town hotel, Bressanone

Elephant

Bressanone is a pretty town at the foot of the Brenner Pass, more Austrian than Italian in character. The same is true of the charming Elephant, named after a beast which was led over the Alps for Emperor Ferdinand of Austria's amusement. The only stable big enough for the exhausted animal was next to the inn, so the innkeeper promptly changed its name to celebrate the event.

There is an air of solid, old-fashioned comfort throughout. Corridors decorated in sumptuous colours are lined with heavily carved and beautifully inlaid antiques. The public rooms are all on the first floor: an elegant 18thC-style sitting room, a large light breakfast room, and three dining rooms. The main one is panelled in dark wood with a vast green ceramic stove and stags' heads on the walls. The food is one of the highlights of a stay here. A reporter commented: 'We had a fabulous dinner; the cooking is imaginative but unfussy with lots of fresh herbs and local ingredients, beautifully presented and bountiful.' Bedrooms are large and comfortable, but disappointing compared with the more characterful public areas. Some have antiques, others have none.

Nearby cathedral; Novacella monastery (3 km).

Via Rio Bianco 4, 39042
Bressanone, Bolzano
Tel 0472 832750
Fax 0472 836579
E-mail elephant.brixen@acs.it
Website www.acs.it/elephant
Location at N end of town; in gardens with parking and garages
Meals breakfast, lunch, dinner
Prices LL
Rooms 44; 28 double and twin, all with bath; 16 single, 15 with bath, one with shower; all rooms have phone, TV, hairdrier
Facilities breakfast room, sitting room, bar, dining rooms, garden, swimming pool, tennis courts
Credit cards AE, DC, MC, V
Disabled 2 ground-floor rooms in annexe
Pets accepted
Closed Nov to Christmas, Jan to Mar
Proprietor Elizabeth Falk

Trentino-Alto Adige

Town hotel, Bressanone

Dominik

This is one of the most unstuffy and relaxing Relais et Châteaux hotels you will find, run with great charm by the Demetz family. The hotel, built in the 1970s, stands on the edge of the oldest part of Bressanone looking out on to the mountains, with the Rienza river running beneath it. Window boxes are filled with geraniums and there is a flowery terrace for dining outdoors. Surrounding the building is a garden of lawns and terraces; inside, it has an open-plan ground floor.

The sitting room has a large open hearth, comfy chairs and coffee tables piled high with magazines, and there are two dining rooms, one cosy and traditional in style, the other contemporary. Bedrooms are modern, very comfortable, and done in bright colours. Fresh flowers and fruit awaits your arrival; the towels are fluffy and generous in size, and bathrooms are capacious.

Our satisfied inspector reports excellent food, with local dishes given an imaginative twist, elegantly presented, and served by helpful, friendly staff. We promoted Dominik from a short to a long entry in the guide: readers' reports would be particularly welcome.

Nearby cathedral; Novacella monastery (3 km).

Via Terzo di Sotto 13, 39042
Bressanone, Bolzano
Tel 0472 830144
Fax 0472 836554
E-mail dominik@pass.dnet.it
Website www.hoteldominik.com
Location on N side of town;
with garage
Meals breakfast, lunch, dinner
Prices LL - LLL
Rooms 36; 25 double and twin,
9 single, 2 suites, all with bath
or shower; all rooms have
phone, TV, minibar,
hairdrier, safe
Facilities sitting room, dining
rooms, bar, terrace, lift, indoor
pool
Credit cards AE, DC, MC, V
Disabled access possible
Pets accepted
Closed Jan to Mar, 3 weeks Nov
Proprietors Demetz family

Trentino-Alto Adige

Country guest-house, Caldaro

Leuchtenburg

This solid stone-built 16thC hostel once housed the servants of Leuchtenburg castle, an arduous hour's trek up the steep wooded mountain behind. Today, guests in the *pensione* are well cared for by the friendly young owners, while the castle lies in ruins. The setting is enviably tranquil, right on Lago di Caldaro, better known (at least to wine buffs) as Kalterer See. Cross a narrow road and you are at the water's edge, where a little private beach is dotted with umbrellas and sunloungers.

Back in the *pensione*, the Sparers provide solid breakfasts and three-course dinners of regional cuisine in an unpretentious, homely atmosphere. White-painted low-arched dining rooms occupy the ground floor; above is the reception, with a large table littered with magazines and surrounded by armchairs. There is another sitting area on the first floor, leading to the bedrooms. These have pretty painted furniture and tiled floors (second-floor rooms are plainer). Each one tells a story: for example, the 'old smoke room' was where food was smoked. All the rooms are large, and some share the views enjoyed from the terrace across vineyards to the lake.

Nearby Swimming and fishing in lake.

Campo di Lago 100, 39052 Caldaro, Bolzano
Tel 0471 960048
Fax 0471 960155
E-mail pensionleuchtenburg@iol.it
Website www.kalterersee.com/pensionleuchtenburg
Location 5 km SE of Caldaro, on the edge of the lake; in courtyard with parking
Meals breakfast, dinner
Prices L
Rooms 19; 15 double and twin, 3 with bath, 12 with shower; 2 single, 2 triple, all with shower; rooms have TV (on request)
Facilities sitting area, dining area, bar, terrace, beach
Credit cards MC, V
Disabled not suitable
Pets accepted
Closed Nov to Easter
Proprietor Markus Sparer

Trentino-Alto Adige

Mountain village hotel, Fié allo Sciliar

Turm

A solid former courthouse dating from the 12thC, with views across pastures and mountains, Hotel Turm offers typical Tyrolean hospitality with style and warmth. Bedrooms are all different and vary considerably in size, but even the smallest has everything you could want for a comfortable stay, including traditional furniture and somewhere cosy to sit. Our inspector's little room was enlivened by a charming group of naïve paintings; another has a working ceramic stove, another a huge pine four-poster. The mini-apartments in particular are excellent value: one, in a little stone tower, is done as a wood-panelled *stübe*, with spiral staircase to a double room and a children's room. The Pramstrahler family's fine collection of contemporary art is displayed in every room and spills out along the whitewashed corridor walls.

The main dining room is light and spacious, with low wood ceiling and windows overlooking the valley; or you can dine in a romantic little room with heavy cast-iron door at the base of the 11thC tower. Either way, the elegantly presented food, cooked by Stefan Pramstrahler, who trained in France, is superb.

Nearby Val Gardena; Bolzano (16 km); Castelrotto (10 km).

Piazza della Chiesa 9, 39050 Fié allo Sciliar, Bolzano
Tel 0471 725014
Fax 0471 725474
E-mail turmwirt@cenida.it
Website www.romantikhotels.com/rhvoels
Location in village, 16 km E of Bolzano, with garden and limited parking
Meals breakfast, lunch, dinner
Prices LL
Rooms 25; 20 double and twin, 6 with bath, 15 with shower; 1 single with shower; 5 apartments with kitchen, 16 with shower, 9 with bath; all rooms have phone, TV, minibar, hairdrier, safe
Facilities sitting room, dining rooms, bar, lift, garden, sauna, indoor and outdoor swimming pools
Credit cards MC, V
Disabled access to public rooms
Pets accepted
Closed Nov to mid-Dec
Proprietor Karl Pramstrahler

Trentino-Alto Adige

Der Pünthof

Via Claudio Augusto, a Roman road to Germany, passed what is now the entrance to Der Pünthof, and the watchtower built to guard the road forms an integral part of the hotel. The main building was a medieval farmhouse and has been in the Wolf family since the 17thC. They opened it as a hotel 40 years ago, housing guests in the barn, but over the decades other buildings have been added. Although Lagundo is a rather dreary suburb of Merano, once inside the hotel's electronic barrier you could be miles from anywhere with only orchards, vineyards and stunning scenery in view.

The public rooms are in the old building: breakfast is served in a pale green *stübe* with wooden floor, low ceiling, ceramic stove and traces of the original decoration on the panelled walls. Bedrooms in the barn are modern and comfortable, but uniform, though some have private terraces on to the garden. The most appealing are the rooms in the square tower. One has polished floorboards, a wood ceiling and antique bed. There are five well-equipped self-catering chalets, and six simpler cheaper rooms in another annexe.

Nearby Bolzano (28 km); Brennero (70 km); Dolomites.

Via Steinach 25, 39022
Lagundo, Bolzano
Tel (0473) 448553
Fax (0473) 449919
Location 3 km NW of Merano, outside village; in own grounds with ample parking
Meals breakfast, dinner
Prices L
Rooms 12 double and twin, 2 with bath, 10 with shower; all rooms have phone, TV, minibar, safe
Facilities 2 breakfast rooms, sitting room, bar, restaurant, sauna, solarium, garden, tennis courts, swimming pool
Credit cards AE, DC, MC, V
Disabled 1 room on ground floor
Pets accepted
Closed Nov to mid-Mar
Proprietors Wolf family

Trentino-Alto Adige

Mountain resort hotel, Marlengo

Oberwirt

The building is typical of the area: solid, whitewashed, red-shuttered, with all sorts of arches and architectural ins and outs, and a crucifix and painted sundial on the front. Inside, public rooms are in traditional Tyrolean style with a profusion of wood panelling, carved furniture and nick-nacks; some bedrooms, however, lack character: comfortable, spacious, mostly with balcony or terrace, but few traditional touches.

Originally a simple inn, Oberwirt has been run by the Waldner family since 1749. Today, three generations currently work in the hotel: Signor Waldner's beaming mother, dressed in a *dirndl*, is at reception, while his daughter runs the restaurant. The hotel is often full, and though it has plenty to recommend it, character and intimacy are not strong features – the misty 'romantic' photo on the cover of the brochure somehow says it all.

The highlight is the food. Our reporter gushed: 'Local produce ... creative presentation ... melt in the mouth pan-fried duck liver, lamb cutlets in a herb crust ... and the best pudding I've ever tasted (well almost): *marscapone* and compote of bitter cherries between wafer thin layers of strudel pastry.'

Nearby Passirio river and valley; Tirolo castle; Dolomites.

Vicolo San Felice 2, Marlengo, 39020 Merano, Bolzano
Tel 0473 222020
Fax 0473 447130
Website www.highlight-hotels.com/oberwirt
Location in village, 4 km SW of Merano; parking in garage or car park
Meals breakfast, lunch, dinner
Prices L
Rooms 40; 34 double and twin, suites and junior suites, 6 single, all with bath or shower; all rooms have phone, TV, minibar, hairdrier, safe
Facilities sitting rooms, dining rooms, bar, meeting room, terrace, garden, indoor and outdoor swimming pools, sauna/solarium, tennis, riding, golf
Credit cards AE, DC, MC, V
Disabled access to public rooms
Pets accepted
Closed mid-Nov to mid-Mar
Proprietor Joseph Waldner and family

Trentino-Alto Adige

Converted castle, Merano

Castel Fragsburg

A lovely drive along a narrow country lane, through mixed woodland and past Alpine pastures, brings you to the east of Merano where Castel Fragsburg – 300 years old and a hotel for more than 100 years – commands splendid views of the Texel massif.

Externally, Fragsburg still looks very much the hunting lodge, with carved wooden shutters and balconies. A terrace along the entire front of the house, covered in wistaria, is a wonderful place to eat or drink: you seem to be suspended over the mountainside. Inside, the adjoining dining room offers Italian, Tyrolean and vegetarian menus and has huge picture windows which open up to become part of the terrace, and you can choose from various Tyrolean-style sitting rooms and a congenial little library. The bedrooms all have balconies, carved pine furniture and colourful country fabrics. The old cellars now contain a sauna and a gym.

The wooded gardens, home to two tame mountain goats, provide plenty of space for lazing – as well as a wooden shelter reserved for all-over suntanning. A great choice for a holiday.
Nearby Promenades along the Passirio river in Merano; Passirio valley; Schloss Rametz; the Dolomites.

Via Fragsburg 3, PO Box 210, 39012 Merano, Bolzano
Tel 0473 244071
Fax 0473 244493
E-mail info@fragsburg.com
Website www.fragsburg.com
Location 6 km NE of Merano; in own gardens with ample parking
Meals breakfast, lunch, dinner
Prices LL
Rooms 18; 13 double and twin, 11 with bath, 2 with shower; 2 single, one with bath, one with shower; 3 suites with bath; all rooms have phone, TV, hairdrier, safe
Facilities sitting rooms, dining rooms, library, sauna, gym, terrace, garden, swimming pool
Credit cards not accepted
Disabled 1 specially adapted room
Pets accepted
Closed Nov to Easter
Proprietors Ortner family

Trentino-Alto Adige

Converted castle, Merano

Castel Labers

On a hillside to the east of Merano, Castel (or Schloss) Labers is immersed in its own lush orchards and vineyards, with direct access to mountain walks through Alpine pastures. The hotel has been in the Neubert family since 1885, but the building itself dates back to the 11thC.

On a bad day, the Castel wouldn't look out of place in an Addams family film, but it has its charm, and the interior is welcoming with an impressive stone staircase with wrought-iron balustrades leading from the arched entrance hall up to the bedrooms. These vary enormously in size and standard: some elegantly proportioned with antique furniture, others rather too drab and basically furnished. The best rooms have balconies, particularly those on the corners; an attic room in the tower with a wood-panelled alcove is also charming.

The castle gardens are packed with trees and flowering shrubs, which can be admired from the conservatory restaurant; there are two other dining rooms, one baronial, with vaulted wooden ceiling. And the ambience? 'Elderly', writes a recent guest. 'Very pleasant, very quiet, but elderly.'

Nearby Passirio river and valley; Tirolo Castle; Dolomites.

Via Labers 25, 39012 Merano, Bolzano
Tel 0473 234484
Fax 0473 234146
Location 2.5 km E of Merano; with private grounds, garage and parking (locked at night)
Meals breakfast, lunch, dinner
Prices LL
Rooms 41; 22 double and twin, 20 with bath, 2 with shower; 9 single, 2 with bath, 7 with shower; 10 family with bath; all rooms have phone, safe; TV on request
Facilities 3 dining rooms, music/reading room, bar, billiard room, conference room, lift, tennis court, swimming pool, garden
Credit cards AE, DC, MC, V
Disabled access difficult
Pets accepted
Closed Nov to April
Proprietors Stapf-Neubert family

Trentino-Alto Adige

Edge-of-town hotel, Merano

Villa Tivoli

Almost in countryside, standing in apple orchards, the pale yellow villa is surrounded by an 'exquisite' terraced garden filled with over 2,000 different plants. Inside all is cool and chic, spacious and light, yet not intimidating. The ground floor is open-plan, with a glass-walled dining room; over the bar an extraordinary contemporary fresco of many-breasted Artemis, a recurring theme in the hotel. Another corner holds a sitting area, elegantly furnished with antiques and there is a traditional wood-panelled Tyrolean *stübe*. Outside, a terrace with tables shaded by yellow umbrellas, and in the basement, a pool room with gaily painted walls. Bedrooms are all different, all comfortable, with south-facing balconies. Some are huge, with separate sitting areas; some are furnished with antiques, others are very contemporary. Bathrooms are large, with double basins. Our reporter was hooked: 'Smart but relaxed; staff warm and welcoming, owners genuinely friendly and aiming to please; mountainous breakfast buffet, designed to see you through till evening, and a delicious dinner (half board includes five courses) accompanied by excellent local wines.'

Nearby Passirio river promenades; Passirio valley; the Dolomites.

Via Verde 72, 39012 Merano, Bolzano
Tel 0473 446282
Fax 0473 446849
E-mail info@villativoli.it
Website www.villativoli.it
Location on edge of town; in own grounds with ample parking
Meals breakfast, lunch, dinner
Prices L
Rooms 21; 14 double, 2 single, all with bath or shower, 5 suites with bath; all rooms have phone, TV, hairdrier
Facilities sitting room, dining room, bar, library, indoor swimming pool, sauna, lift, terrace, garden
Credit cards AE, DC, MC, V
Disabled access difficult
Pets accepted
Closed mid-Dec to mid-Mar
Proprietors Defranceschi family

Trentino-Alto Adige

Converted castle, Missiano

Schloss Korb

Rising up above the fertile vineyards and orchards that surround the outskirts of Bolzano is the 11thC tower which forms the centrepiece of Schloss Korb.

The entrance to the hotel is a riot of colour – flowering shrubs and plants set against walls of golden stone and whitewash. Inside, furnishings and decorations are in traditional style, and antiques and fresh flowers abound. Reception is a cool, dark, tiled hall set about with a most eccentric collection of objects including carvings, golden angels on the walls, huge plants, busts, heavy mirrors, brass ornaments and armoury – the oldest part of the hotel. Surrounding the main restaurant is a terrace, hanging out over the valley and awash with plants, where breakfast and drinks can be enjoyed. The feel of the place is relaxed, though not intimate.

The bedrooms in the castle are generous in size, with separate sitting areas and lovely views out over the vineyards. Best are those in the tower, or the traditional apartment with its carved furniture. Rooms in the annexe all have balconies, and here there is a lift and an indoor heated pool.

Nearby Bolzano (8 km); Merano (36 km); Dolomites.

Missiano, 39050 San Paolo, Bolzano
Tel 0471 636000
Fax 0471 636033
E-mail hotel-schloss-korb@dnet.it
Website www.highlight-hotels.com/korb
Location 8 km W of Bolzano, in gardens; ample parking
Meals breakfast, lunch, dinner
Prices L
Rooms 62; 54 double and twin, 2 single, all with bath; 6 suites, 5 with bath, one with shower; all rooms have phone, TV; half the rooms have safe
Facilities sitting rooms, dining room, bar, sauna, beauty salon, conference rooms, terraces, garden, tennis courts, indoor and outdoor swimming pools
Credit cards not accepted
Disabled access difficult
Pets accepted
Closed Nov to Mar
Proprietors Dellago family

Trentino-Alto Adige

Mountain chalet, Ortisei

Uhrerhof Deur

The name means 'House of the Clocks', and their ticking and chiming, along with birdsong, are very often the only sounds which break the silence at this traditional chalet set in a tucked-away hamlet 1,600 metres above sea level. Indeed, noise levels hardly rise above a whisper, and Signora Zemmer is at pains to point out that this is a place only for those seeking total peace and quiet. Outside, there is a grassy garden from which to enjoy the wide and wonderful view. Inside, all the rooms, including the balconied bedrooms, are bright, simple and beautifully kept, with plenty of homely details. The core of the chalet is 400 years old, and includes the all-wood *stübe* with working stove. The three adjoining dining rooms have wooden benches round the walls, Tyrolean fabrics for curtains and cushions, bright rugs on terracotta floors and pewter plates displayed in wall racks. Signor Zemmer is the chef, and his simple yet delicious food is elegantly presented on pewter plates.

Underneath the house is a surprisingly smart health complex, with huge picture windows so that you can relax in the open-plan Turkish bath and soak up the view.

Nearby Val Gardena; Castelrotto (13 km); Bolzano (26 km).

Bulla, 39046 Ortisei, Bolzano
Tel 0471 797335
Fax 0471 797457
Fax uhrerhof@val-gardena.com
Website
www.val-gardena.com/hotel/uhrerhof
Location in mountainside hamlet, 13 km E of Castelrotto, off Castelrotto–Ortisei road; garage parking
Meals breakfast, dinner
Prices L-LL
Rooms 11; 5 double and twin, 4 with bath, 1 with shower; 2 single with shower; 4 apartments for 2 to 5 people with kitchen, living room; all rooms have phone, TV, hairdrier, safe
Facilities dining room, bar, sitting room, garden, health centre
Credit cards MC, V
Disabled not suitable
Pets not accepted
Closed Nov, 2 weeks after Easter
Proprietors Zemmer family

Trentino-Alto Adige

Converted castle, Pergine

Castel Pergine

This medieval hilltop fortress is managed with love and enthusiasm by an energetic and cultured Swiss couple, Verena and Theo. Past and present coexist happily in a rather alternative atmosphere, and the castle has a truly lived-in feel despite its grand dimensions and impressive history. A recent visit confirmed that this is one of the most affordable and distinctive hotels in the entire region.

The route from the car park to the hotel leads you under stone arches, up age-worn steps and through vaulted chambers to the airy, round reception hall where breakfast is also served. The two spacious dining rooms afford wonderful views, and the cooking, based on the regional cuisine, is light and innovative. The bedrooms are by no means luxurious, and some are very small, but all are furnished in simple good taste; the best have splendid, heavy, carved wooden furniture and wall panelling.

One of the most enchanting features of the castle is the walled garden. Spend an hour reading a book, or simply watching the mountains through the crumbling ramparts, and you may never want to leave.

Nearby Trento (11 km); Lake Caldonazzo (3 km); Segonzano.

38057 Pergine, Valsugana, Trento
Tel 0461 531158
Fax 0461 531329
E-mail castelpergine@valsugana.com
Location off the SS47 Padua road, 2 km SE of Pergine; in own grounds with ample parking
Meals breakfast, dinner
Prices L
Rooms 21; 13 double and twin, 8 with shower; 4 single, 3 with shower; 4 triple, 3 with shower; all rooms have phone
Facilities sitting room, dining rooms, bar, garden
Credit cards AE, MC, V
Disabled access difficult
Pets accepted
Closed Nov to Thursday before Easter
Proprietors Verena and Theo Schneider-Neff

Trentino-Alto Adige

Converted castle, Rasun di Sopra

Ansitz Heufler

The word 'ansitz' means unfortified aristocratic residence and this one, dating from the 16thC, is a beautiful example. Although set rather incongruously on the edge of an unremarkable village, it is surrounded by stunning scenery. The hotel has featured in our all-Italy guide for many years, but has recently changed hands. Our inspector felt that though alterations made by the new owners are subtle, they are not all beneficial. The rooms look fresh, but some have been changed around so that the main sitting room, a superbly carved old *stübe*, is now practically devoid of furniture and only used for receptions. The profusion of beribboned candles, lace cushions and teddy bears in alcoves were too pretty-pretty for her taste.

The food served in the three wood-panelled dining rooms is no longer solid Tyrolean fare, but leans strongly towards the *nouvelle*. The bar is in the original smokery with blackened walls and vaulted ceiling. The bedrooms are all different, full of marvellous furniture and architectural features, but beware of hitting your head on low lintels. A lovely hotel, whose soul has unfortunately been compromised by the recent prettifying.

Nearby Brunico (10 km).

Rasun di Sopra 37, 39030
Rasun, Anterselva
Tel 0474 498582
Fax 0474 498046
E-mail ansitz-heufler@dnet.it
Location in village in wooded Anterselva valley, 10 km E of Brunico; in own grounds with parking
Meals breakfast, lunch, dinner
Prices LL
Rooms 8; 5 double and twin, 2 with bath, 3 with shower; 3 suites, 2 with bath, 1 with
shower; all rooms have phone
Facilities sitting rooms, sitting areas, dining rooms, bar, garden,
Credit cards AE, DC, MC, V
Disabled not suitable
Pets not accepted
Closed mid-Nov to Dec, mid-Apr to May
Proprietor Johann Oberhammer

Trentino-Alto Adige

Mountain hotel, Redagno di Sopra

Zirmerhof

Situated just outside the tiny hamlet of Redagno di Sopra, this 12thC *mas* has been in the Perwanger family since 1890. Views are of mountains, green pastures and forests with few signs of civilization to mar the landscape. "I Dyllic", a recent guest tells us. The interior has been carefully restored. The dim, low-ceilinged hall with its intricate wood carving, ticking grandfather clock and old fireplace, immediately plunges you into the atmosphere of an old family home. There is a tiny cosy library, a sitting-cum-breakfast room with an open fire for winter days, and a rustic bar with a grassy terrace, from which to enjoy the superb views. The large wood-panelled dining room houses two elaborate ceramic stoves, and makes a fine setting in which to enjoy the local dishes and sophisticated wines on offer.

The comfortable bedrooms vary enormously in size, but all are attractive with traditional carved furniture (much of it made on the premises) and pretty fabrics; the largest rooms are on the top floor. For the energetic, there's plenty to do, particularly in winter, from skating and curling on the lake to cross-country and downhill skiing. A pool and health complex opens soon.
Nearby Cavalese (15 km).

39040 Redagno, Bolzano
Tel 0471 887215
Fax 0471 887225
E-mail info@zirmerhof.com
Website www.zirmerhof.com
Location 5 km N of Fontanefredde, off the SS48; in garden with ample parking
Meals breakfast, lunch, dinner
Prices L-LL
Rooms 31; 23 double and twin, 2 with bath, 21 with shower; 7 single, 2 with bath, 5 with shower; 1 suite with shower;

rooms have TV on request
Facilities dining room, sitting room, bar, library, garden
Credit cards AE, DC, MC, V
Disabled ground-floor bedrooms available
Pets accepted
Closed early Nov to day after Christmas, after Easter to mid-May
Proprietor Sepp Perwanger

Trentino-Alto Adige

Country guest-house, San Osvaldo

Gasthof Tschötscherhof

Don't be put off by the unpronounceable name; for lovers of simple, farmhouse accommodation in an unspoilt rural setting, this hostelry could be ideal. The narrow road from Siusi winds through apple orchards, vineyards and open meadows, eventually arriving at the tiny hamlet of San Osvaldo and this typical 500-year-old farmhouse with its adjacent dark wood barn. The name, painted on the outside of the building, is almost hidden by the clambering vines, and the old wooden balconies are a colourful riot of cascading geraniums. The sun-drenched terrace is a perfect spot for relaxing and eating.

Inside, we were assailed by inviting smells from the kitchen at the end of the hall, and were drawn to the warmth of the low-ceilinged old *stübe* with its gently ticking clock, rough wood floor and simple white ceramic stove.

A rustic stone stairway leads up to the modest but tidy bedrooms, some of which have balconies. They have no frills, but after a long day in glorious countryside, we were too tired to notice on our return.

Nearby Castelrotto (5 km); Bolzano (17 km); Sciliar Natural Park (10 km).

San Osvaldo 19, 39040 Siuisi, Bolzano
Tel 0471 706013
Fax 0471 704801
E-mail tschoetscherhof@rolmail.net
Location in hamlet, 5 km W of Castelrotto; with parking
Meals breakfast, lunch, dinner
Prices L
Rooms 8; 7 double and twin, 1 single, all with shower
Facilities dining rooms, terrace
Credit cards not accepted
Disabled access difficult

Pets accepted
Closed Dec to Mar
Proprietors Jaider family

Trentino-Alto Adige

Mountain guest-house, San Valburga d'Ultimo

Eggwirt

The quiet and unspoilt Val d'Ultima lies 30 kilometres south-west of Merano. An ideal setting for both summer and winter sports, the Gasthof Eggwirt has existed as a hostelry since the 14thC, and today the Schwienbacher family welcome guests as if to their own home. The hotel is on the edge of the village with a large terrace at the front and superb views all around. The long life of the house is best felt in the *stübe* which dates from 1611: entirely panelled in dark wood with an old ceramic stove in the corner and stags' heads on the walls, this room was a favourite haunt of Sir Herbert Dunhill (a regular guest), and his black and white photographs are on display. A larger room housing a little bar has a country feel to it, with a ticking clock and rough, bare floorboards (which are scrubbed daily).

Upstairs, the decoration is more modern, less personal. The bright bedrooms have lots of wood and cheerful duvet covers. Some of the larger ones are divided, and most have balconies with, of course, stunning views. We should mention that this inexpensive, relaxed and friendly family hotel offers some excellent ski deals for the children.

Nearby Merano (30 km).

39016 San Valburga d'Ultimo, Bolzano
Tel 0473 795319
Fax 0473 795471
E-mail eggwirt@rolmail.net
Website www.ultenfal.it
Location 35 km SW of Merano, off SS238, in village; parking
Meals breakfast, lunch, dinner
Prices L
Rooms 20; 11 double and twin, 10 with shower, 1 with bath; 3 single with shower; 4 triple, 2 with bath, 2 with shower, 2 family with shower; all rooms have phone, TV on request, safe
Facilities restaurant, sitting room, bar, terraces
Credit cards not accepted
Disabled not suitable
Pets accepted
Closed 10 Nov to 24 Dec
Proprietor Schwienbacher family

Trentino-Alto Adige

Mountain hotel, Siusi allo Sciliar

Bad Ratzes

Leaving the small town of Siusi in search of Bad Ratzes, the road winds uphill past green meadows and into a dense forest where Hansel and Gretel would have felt at home. When at last you reach it in a clearing, the hotel, large and modern, looks disconcertingly grim, but the warmth and enthusiasm of the Scherlin sisters will put you immediately at ease. Inside, the decoration is dull 1960s and 1970s, but comfortable. Public areas – including a formal sitting room with open fireplace, a children's playroom, and two dining rooms – are extensive. All but four of the spotless bedrooms have balconies.

Food is important at Bad Ratzes: local dishes are carefully prepared and pasta is home-made. One of the sisters bakes regularly, and her recipes are recorded in a little booklet. This is one of a group of family hotels in the area and there are many thoughtful child-orientated extras: pots of crayons and paper on the dining tables, a booklet of local bedtime stories, walks for children, a special menu and so on. Adults are not neglected; there is wonderful and varied walking in the neighbourhood and a free ski bus runs to the slopes in winter.

Nearby Bolzano (22 km); Siusi National Park; skiing (10 km).

Bagnidi Razzes, 39040 Siusi allo Sciliar, Bolzano
Tel (0471) 706131
Fax (0471) 706131
Location 22 km NE of Bolzano, 3 km SE of Siusi; in own grounds with ample parking
Meals breakfast, lunch, dinner
Prices L
Rooms 52; 36 double, 9 single, 7 family rooms, all with bath; all rooms have phone, hairdrier; 18 rooms have TV and safe
Facilities dining rooms, sitting rooms, bar, playroom, indoor swimming pool, sauna, garden, garage
Credit cards not accepted
Disabled not suitable
Pets accepted
Closed Sunday after Easter to mid-May
Proprietors Scherlin family

Trentino-Alto Adige

Town hotel, Trento

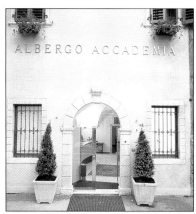

Accademia

Favoured by showbiz types, this upmarket hotel is run by two lively sisters and their efficient staff, and occupies an attractive medieval house on a tiny street in the old centre of Trento. Quaint wooden shutters and geranium-filled window boxes break up the four storeys of elegant cream stucco façade. Inside, elements of the original architecture are also visible: a stone stairway leading up from reception, doorways and vaulted ceilings. The building's clean white lines are enlivened by vibrant rugs, parquet floors and strategically placed antiques.

The atmosphere is carried through to the bright, airy bedrooms, decorated predominantly in blue and white. Some have a rustic air, varnished wood floors and attic ceilings. The wood-panelled suite at the top is particularly appealing, furnished with smart modern sofas, colourful kilims and modern prints.

The restaurant – a white vaulted room, with crisp tablecloths – serves interesting, creative food. There is also a homely *enoteca*, where you can taste a wide range of local wines or have a snack. Breakfast is a particular pleasure when taken on the walled terrace, shaded by a giant horse-chestnut tree.

Nearby Santa Maria; Piazza del Duomo.

Vicolo Colico 4–6, 38100 Trento
Tel 0461 233600
Fax 0461 230174
Location in old part of town between Duomo and Piazza Dante; with free parking nearby
Meals breakfast, lunch, dinner
Prices L-LL
Rooms 43; 32 double and twin, 16 with bath, 16 with shower; 9 single with shower; 2 suites with bath; all rooms have phone, TV, air-conditioning, minibar,
hairdrier
Facilities sitting rooms, restaurant, *enoteca*, terrace
Credit cards AE, DC, MC, V
Disabled no special facilities
Pets accepted
Closed Christmas to early Jan, restaurant Monday
Proprietors Fambri family

San Marco

Town hotel

Alcyone

Recently renovated, this was formerly an old-fashioned *pensione* called the Brooklyn. Though the new owners are proud of their make-over, one suspects that the old hotel had more character because the parts which have been left intact are charming. The pretty little breakfast room has waist-high painted panelling with gold velvet above, dotted with ceramic plates; the stairwell is similar. The newly decorated sugar-almond pink bedrooms are very small, done out in standard Venice hotel style: purpose made painted furniture, Murano glass wall lights, silk damask bedcovers. Prices are ambitious.

Nearby Piazza San Marco; San Zulian.

Calle dei Fabbri, San Marco 4712, 30124 Venezia **Tel** (041) 5212508 **Fax** (041) 5212942 **Location** in shopping street, 2 mins walk from Piazza San Marco; **vaporetto** San Marco, Rialto or water taxi **Meals** breakfast **Prices** rooms L90,000–L280,000; standard double	L280,000; breakfast included **Rooms** 21; 19 double and twin, 2 single, 2 with bath, 19 with shower; all rooms have phone, TV, air-conditioning, hairdrier **Facilities** breakfast room **Children** accepted **Disabled** not suitable **Pets** accepted **Closed** never **Proprietor** Alessio Ricchi

---

Town hotel

Bel Sito & Berlino

The Bel Sito has its charms, including a flowery patio right on the *campo*, and given a sympathetic facelift one feels it could make a fine hotel. Too many of the rooms, however (they vary greatly), are small, skimpily furnished and worn at the edges, and the extensive reception rooms look dowdy (although the long, mirrored breakfast room retains its old-fashioned dignity). Nos 30 and 40 have little balconies and wonderful close-up views of the exuberant baroque façade of Santa Maria Zobenigo, but they need updating and redecoration. Best are the rooms with views on to the canal.

Nearby Piazza San Marco; Teatro La Fenice.

Campo Santa Maria del Giglio, San Marco 2517, 30124 Venezia **Tel** (041) 5223365 **Fax** (041) 5204083 **Location** between Piazza San Marco and Campo Santo Stefano; **vaporetto** Santa Maria del Giglio or water taxi **Meals** breakfast **Prices** rooms L115,000–L347,000; standard double L190,000–L275,000; breakfast included **Rooms** 38	double, twin, triple and single, all with bath or shower; all rooms have phone, TV, hairdrier; air-conditioning units on request **Facilities** sitting room, breakfast room, bar, terrace **Credit cards** AE, MC, V **Children** accepted **Disabled** access difficult **Pets** accepted **Closed** never **Proprietor** Luigi Gino Serafini

San Marco

Town-house apartment

Ca' San Vidal

If modern sophistication rather than local colour is preferred when looking for self-catering, this family apartment could be the answer. On the first floor, right by the Accademia Bridge, light streams through floor-length windows on two sides of its elegant sitting room.

The principal bedroom, with king-size bed, is all white, trimmed with red *toile de jouey*. A slip of a room has a *bateau lit* and another, bathed in golden yellow, has two single beds. Bathrooms are 'international' in style, all black marble, with fearsome looking jacuzzis. New to the guide.

Nearby Accademia gallery; Piazza San Marco.

Contact Venetian Apartments, 413 Parkway House, Sheen Lane, London SW14.
Tel (0181) 878 1130
Fax (0181) 878 0982
E-mail enquiries@venice-rentals.com
Website www.venice-rentals.com
Location between Accademia bridge and Campo Santo Stefano, close to the Grand Canal; vaporetto Accademia

Prices apartment £1,750 per week (minium rental one week)
Rooms 2 double, one single bedroom, sitting room, kitchen, 2 bathrooms; phone, TV, air-conditioning, maid service
Disabled lift; no special facilities
Pets not accepted
Closed never

Town hotel

Centauro

A hotel that has been in existence since the 17thC, and in the Tomasutti family for much of the 20thC. Riccardo has broken away from tradition however, and transformed what was a slightly dingy two star. Flock wallpaper has been jettisoned in favour of glossy paint effects; beams have been washed dark red with a yellow motif; the huge doors painted pale green. The cavernous breakfast room, freshly painted in yellow and white, still has its original parquet floor. Bedrooms, six with canal views, are airy with white walls, high ceilings, Venetian marble floors and fabric-covered furniture.

Nearby Bovolo staircase; Teatro La Fenice; Rialto Bridge.

Calle D. Vida, Campo Manin, San Marco 4297/a, 30124 Venezia
Tel 041 5225832
Fax 041 5239151
E-mail centauro@hotelcentauro.com
Website www.hotelcentauro.com
Location in little street to the S of the square; **vaporetto** Rialto
Meals LL
Rooms 31; 18 double and twin, all with bath or shower; 6 single with shower; 6 triple and family, 1 suite, all with bath or shower; all rooms have phone, TV, minibar **Facilities** breakfast room, sitting area **Credit cards** AE, DC, MC, V
Disabled not suitable
Pets accepted
Closed Nov to Jan
Proprietor Ricardo Tomasutti

San Marco

Town hotel

Do Pozzi

In a tiny palm-fringed courtyard, where café tables and chairs spill on to the pavement in summer, this hotel has the twin advantages of a quiet central location and its own restaurant, 'da Raffaele', specializing in Venetian cuisine and prettily set on a side canal. But our inspector's high expectations were disappointed by the dull interior; acres of silk damask cover the walls and furnishings are standard throughout. She regretted that there were not more original touches like the icons in the outer breakfast room. Bedrooms are serviceabl; some have been given a much-needed revamp. Bathrooms are 'excruciatingly small'.
Nearby Santa Maria del Giglio; Teatro La Fenice.

Calle Larga 22 Marzo, San Marco 2373, 30124 Venezia
Tel 041 5207855
Fax 041 5229413
Location in courtyard S of Calle Larga 22 Marzo; **vaporetto** Santa Maria del Giglio, San Marco
Meals breakfast
Prices LL
Rooms 30; 25 double and twin, all with bath or shower; 5 single with shower; all rooms have phone, TV, air-conditioning, minibar, hairdrier
Facilities 2 breakfast/sitting rooms, restaurant, lift **Credit cards** AE, DC, MC, V **Children** accepted **Disabled** no special facilities **Pets** accepted
Closed never
Proprietor Stefania Salmaso

Town hotel

Kette

Refurbished a few years ago in an ambitiously formal style of faux marble and much wood panelling, the Kette now has a disappointingly institutional feel. Displays of Murano glass and a few *objets d'art* add some personality. Bedrooms are traditional, with a masculine touch – dark wood furniture, carved headboards, parquet floors, striped wallpaper, plain or paisley fabrics. At the time of our inspector's visit work was under way on a large new ground-floor breakfast room, which replaces an elegant room on the second floor. The hotel is ideally positioned, backing on to a canal near Campo San Fantin.
Nearby Teatro La Fenice; Piazza San Marco.

Piscina San Moisè, San Marco 2053, 30124 Venezia
Tel 041 5207766
Fax 041 5228964
E-mail info@hotelkette.com
Website www.hotelkette.com
Location 5 mins walk from Piazza San Marco, near Campo San Fantin; **vaporetto** San Marco or water taxi
Meals breakfast
Prices LLL
Rooms 65; 58 double, twin and triple, 7 single, all with bath or shower; all rooms have phone, TV, air-conditioning, minibar, hairdrier, safe
Facilities breakfast room, TV room, lift **Credit cards** AE, DC, MC, V **Disabled** access difficult
Pets accepted **Closed** never
Proprietor Signor Baessato

San Marco

Town hotel

Monaco & Grand Canal

A traditional grand hotel with all the trappings including plush Venetian-style furnishings, impeccably uniformed footmen, and multilingual receptionists, who are perfectly charming so long as you're a VIP. Its attractions are the location, right on the Grand Canal, with magical views across to Salute and San Giorgio Maggiore, masses of space downstairs to sit in comfortable armchairs and enjoy them, and a sophisticated, intimate restaurant. The drawback, we've heard, is noise from *vaporetti* chugging past, which disturbs the first-floor rooms at the front. Go for a room – or suite, if you can afford it – on an upper floor.
Nearby Piazza San Marco.

Calle Vallaresso, San Marco 1325, 30124 Venezia
Tel 041 5200211
Fax 041 5200501
E-mail mailbox@hotelmonaco.it
Location right on Grand Canal to W of Piazza San Marco; **vaporetto** San Marco **Meals** breakfast, lunch, dinner
Prices LLLL
Rooms 70; 64 double and twin and single, 6 suites, all with bath; all rooms have phone, TV, air-conditioning, minibar, hairdrier, safe
Facilities breakfast room, sitting rooms, restaurant, bar, lift, terrace **Credit cards** AE, DC, MC, V **Disabled** no special facilities **Pets** accepted
Closed never
Manager Giuseppe Vacciano

Apartments

Palazzo del Giglio

This handsome converted mansion contains 19 smart flats to rent on a daily or weekly basis. Size varies from one-room studios to a penthouse that sleeps five with a roof terrace (No. 401). Price depends not just on the size of the apartment and length of your stay, but also on the time of year, number of people, and whether it has a view. All elegantly decorated in a similar style, the comfortable rooms are well furnished with a mix of the traditional and the ultra-modern. Cleverly designed kitchens are tucked into tiny spaces. Bathrooms are of sparkling Carrara marble, some with jacuzzis.
Nearby Santa Maria del Giglio; Teatro La Fenice.

Campo Santa Maria del Giglio, San Marco, 30124 Venezia
Tel 041 2719111
Fax 041 5205158
E-mail gmariani@giglio.it
Location just N of the Gritti Palace; **vaporetto** Santa Maria del Giglio
Meals room-service breakfast
Prices LLL-LLLL
Rooms 19 apartments: studio, one-bedroom and two-bedroom; all apartments have phone, TV, fax/modem point, air-conditioning, kitchen, hairdrier, safe
Facilities maid service
Credit cards AE, DC, MC, V
Disabled no special facilities
Pets accepted
Closed never
Manager Maria Elena Fabiano

San Marco

Panada

The real attraction of this hotel is its bar. A couple of guests we met here agreed, saying it was the perfect place for a nightcap. Cosy and wood-panelled, with red velvet seats, it lives up to its name 'Ai Speci' ('of mirrors' in local dialect), as almost every inch of wall space is covered by antique looking-glasses. The hotel itself tends towards predictability. Pluses are a decent-sized and comfortable sitting area, and freshly decorated bedrooms with attractive painted furniture. Minuses are a staff who could muster only a cool welcome and an easy win in any 'most hideous breakfast room' contest.

Nearby Piazza San Marco; San Zulian.

Calle Specchieri, San Marco 646, 30124 Venezia
Tel 041 5209088
Fax 041 5209619
E-mail htlpanve@spacehotels.it
Location between Calle Larga San Marco and San Zulian; **vaporetto** San Marco
Meals breakfast
Prices LLL
Rooms 48; 28 double and twin, 7 triple and family, 13 single, all with bath or shower; all rooms have phone, TV, air-conditioning, hairdrier, safe
Facilities breakfast room, bar, sitting room, lift
Credit cards AE, DC, MC, V
Disabled no special facilities
Pets accepted
Closed never
Manager Maurizio Scarpa

Torino

A fine Gothic façade, flaunting splendid ogee windows, some impressive stuccoed ceilings, and a fusty feel are the last traces of the original 15thC *palazzo*. On the whole, the Torino is low-key by *palazzo* standards, with predictable decoration and modern furnishings. In keeping with its history, however, are the medieval-style reception desk, and the saintly statue which watches over guests as they eat a frugal breakfast. Bedrooms vary from huge, high-ceilinged first-floor rooms with swirling carpets and tall windows, to smaller, cosier pink rooms on the upper floors with rooftop views.

Nearby Santa Maria del Giglio; Teatro La Fenice.

Calle delle Ostreghe, San Marco 2356, 30124 Venezia
Tel 041 5205222
Fax 041 5228227
E-mail info@hoteltorino.it
Website www.hoteltorino.it
Location just W of Campo Santa Maria del Giglio; **vaporetto** Santa Maria del Giglio, San Marco
Meals breakfast
Prices LL
Rooms 20; 19 double and twin, 1 single, all with shower; all rooms have phone, TV, air-conditioning, minibar, hairdrier, safe **Facilities** breakfast room, sitting area
Credit cards AE, DC, MC, V
Disabled not possible
Pets accepted **Closed** never
Manager Ludovico Moro

San Marco

Town hotel

San Giorgio

If you want a quiet location, yet close to the bustling main thoroughfare between San Marco and Rialto, consider the San Giorgio, tucked down a side street next to the Museo Fortuny. Bedrooms are small, neat, well cared for, with bathrooms of varying sizes, some with large shower cubicles. One room has an attractive carved wardrobe, others have pretty examples of Venetian painted furniture. Downstairs is a large, rather dark sitting/breakfast room. While unremarkable, this is another example of a simple two-star hotel which gives better value for money than many a more expensive three star.

Nearby Piazza San Marco; Accademia gallery.

Rio Terrà della Mandola, San Marco 3781, 30124 Venezia
Tel 041 5235835
Fax 041 5228072
Location off Calle della Mandola, close to Campo Sant' Angelo, between San Marco & Rialto; **vaporetto** Sant'Angelo
Meals breakfast
Prices L-LL
Rooms 16; 12 double/twin, 4

single, all with shower; all rooms have phone, TV, air-conditioning, hairdrier, safe
Facilities sitting/ breakfast room
Credit cards AE, MC, V
Disabled not suitable
Pets accepted
Closed never
Proprietor Renzo Cristofoli Prat

Town guest-house

San Zulian

A little hotel where public rooms and corridors are painted white, with colourful pictures and neat furniture and fittings. Bedrooms, though simple, are similarly fresh, well-equipped, with pretty green furniture and white tiled bathrooms with properly enclosed showers. Rooms vary in size, so try for a larger one. Only one breaks the mould, with a silk hanging above the bed and a charming ottoman at its foot. The 'honeymoon room' has a private terrace with views across the rooftops to the domes of San Marco (which helps to compensate for the minute bathroom).

Nearby San Zulian; Santa Maria Formosa; Piazza San Marco.

Piscina San Zulian, San Marco 535, 30124 Venezia
Tel 041 5225872
Fax 041 5232265
E-mail h.sanzulian@italyhotel.com
Website
www.venere/it/venezia/san_zulian
Location beside San Zulian church, between Piazza San Marco and Rialto; **vaporetto** San Marco**Meals** breakfast

Prices LL
Rooms 19, all double and twin or triple, all with shower; all rooms have phone, TV, air-conditioning, minibar, hairdrier, safe
Facilities breakfast/sitting room
Credit cards AE, DC, MC, V
Children accepted **Disabled** not suitable **Pets** accepted **Closed** never **Proprietor** Mauro Girotto

Santa Croce

Town hotel

Falier

In a lively university neighbourhood, where students throng the streets, this well-placed straightforward two star is under the same ownership as the American (see page 52). Though lacking the character and flair of its better known sister, the Falier is decorated to a high standard. Pleasant public rooms are done out in subtle shades, with marble chequered floors, and there's a pretty terracotta-tiled courtyard for *al fresco* breakfasts. Identical-looking bedrooms have innocuous modern fittings, but there's one at the top with beams and a private roof terrace. At the same price as a standard double, it's a bargain.

Nearby Scuola Grande di San Rocco; Frari.

Salizzada San Pantalon, Santa Croce 130, 30135 Venezia	**Rooms** 19; 14 double and twin, 5 single, all with shower; all rooms have phone, hairdrier
Tel 041 710882/711005	
Fax 041 5206554	**Facilities** breakfast room, sitting area, garden
E-mail falier@tin.it	
Website www.hotelfalier.com	**Credit cards** AE, MC, V
Location just W of the San Pantalon canal; **vaporetto** Piazzale Roma, San Tomà	**Disabled** no special facilities
	Pets accepted
	Closed never
Meals breakfast	**Proprietor** Salvatore Sutera Sardo
Prices LL	

Town hotel

Al Sole

This hotel occupies the 16thC *palazzo* Ca' Marcello, a lovely mellow brick buiding with narrow Gothic arches for windows, built on the dog-leg in the Rio dei Tolentini. The best bedrooms afford views down both stretches of the canal. Relics from its *palazzo* days include beamed ceilings supported by stone columns, and chequerboard marble floors. Unfortunately most of the furnishings date from 1971, when it was converted to a hotel – or look as if they do – and the bedrooms are drab. But there's a jolly bar on the ground floor with doors leading to a very pretty vine-shaded garden.

Nearby Scuola Grande di San Rocco; Frari.

Fondamenta Minotto, Santa Croce 136, 30135 Venezia	**Rooms** 80; 63 double and twin, 17 single, all with bath or shower; all rooms have phone, TV, air-conditioning, minibar, hairdrier **Facilities** sitting areas, bar, restaurant, lift, garden
Tel 041 710844	
Fax 041 714398	
E-mail info@corihotels.it	
Website www.corihotels.it	
Location opposite Tolentini bridge; **vaporetto** Piazzale Roma or water taxi	**Credit cards** AE, DC, MC, V
	Disabled no special facilities
	Pets accepted
	Closed never
Meals breakfast, dinner	**Manager** Mario Scarpa
Prices LL	

Castello

Town hotel

Canada

Two rooms only are worth having here: the ones at the very top, each with its own wooden railed terrace looking out across tiled roofs and church façades to the *campanile* of St Mark's. Though simple and straightforward, their carved mahogany and studded velvet bedheads add a touch of pomp, and the bathrooms are clean and neat. They cost no more than any other room, but the bonus of the terrace makes them distinctly good value. You will have to climb endless stairs to reach reception, and yet more to get to the bedrooms so only the fit need apply. A simple hotel with some character; we found the staff friendly.

Nearby Rialto; Santa Maria Formosa.

Campo San Lio, Castello 5659, 30122 Venezia
Tel 041 5229912
Fax 041 5235852
Location in small square, midway between Rialto and Campo Santa Maria Formosa **vaporetto** Rialto
Meals breakfast
Prices LL
Rooms 25, all double and twin, 4 with bath, 21 with shower; all rooms have phone
Facilities breakfast room
Credit cards MC, V
Disabled not suitable
Pets accepted
Closed never
Proprietor Signor Brusaferro

Town hotel

Paganelli

This modest, friendly place gives itself no airs at all – in fact the wood-veneer-clad entrance, filled with leather chairs, looks remarkably unprepossessing – but it shares the same lagoon views as much more august and expensive hotels on the Riva. And the simple pleasant bedrooms far exceed the public rooms. They are furnished with pretty, delicate, painted pieces, and gauze curtains flutter at the shuttered windows. Largest and smartest rooms face the waterfront: No. 6 is our favourite. Breakfast is served in an annexe in the adjoining side street, where a number of bedrooms are also located.

Nearby San Zaccaria; Piazza San Marco.

Riva degli Schiavoni, Castello 4182, 30122 Venezia
Tel 041 5224324 **Fax** 041 5239267 **Location** between Sott. Calle San Zaccaria and Rio dei Greci; **vaporetto** San Zaccaria
Meals breakfast
Prices LL
Rooms 22; 20 double and twin, triple and family, 16 with bath or shower; 2 single, one with shower; all rooms have phone, TV, air-conditioning, safe
Facilities sitting area, breakfast room
Credit cards AE, MC, V
Disabled one room on ground floor
Pets not accepted
Closed never
Proprietors Francesco and Giorgio Paganelli

Castello

Town guest-house

Pensione Wildner

Two long-standing budget options tucked between the four-star palaces along the Riva degli Schiavoni are the Paganelli (see above) and the Pensione Wildner. The same family has run the Wildner for over 35 years, maintaining an air of solid respectability amid the hubbub of the waterfront. All the bedrooms are similar in their old-fashioned simplicity, but the ones to try for are those with a view across the lagoon which are no more expensive than the rest. Some can sleep four, which makes a useful option for families or friends on a budget.

Nearby San Zaccaria; Piazza San Marco; San Giovanni in Bragora.

Riva degli Schiavoni, Castello 4161, 30122 Venezia **Tel** 041 5227463 **Fax** 041 5265615 **Location** on the waterfront between Ponte del Vin and Ponte dei Greci, close to Piazza San Marco **vaporetto** San Zaccaria, San Marco **Meals** breakfast, lunch, dinner **Prices** LL	**Rooms** 16 double and twin, triple or family with shower; all rooms have phone, TV, air-conditioning, safe **Facilities** breakfast room, bar, restaurant **Credit cards** AE, DC, MC, V **Disabled** not suitable **Pets** accepted **Closed** never **Proprietor** Nicola Fullin

Town-house apartments

San Simeon

A nondescript door in an alley just off the mighty Riva degli Schiavoni leads to these three thoughtfully decorated one-bedroom apartments, perfect for a romantic twosome. (For families, an extra sofa bed in each could accommodate one or two small children.) The apartments, opened in 1996, belong to the Ai Due Fanali hotel (see page 49), and there is a direct line to the hotel if you need information or help. Two apartments enjoy fabulous views across the lagoon. Breakfast is provided each morning as well as maid service; dinner can also be shopped for and cooked at extra cost.

Nearby Piazza San Marco; Arsenale; San Giovanni in Bragora.

For information contact: Ai Due Fanali, Santa Croce 946, 30135 Venice **Tel** 041 718490 **Fax** 041 718344 **Location** off Riva degli Schiavoni between La Pietà and Ponte Ca' di Dio **vaporetto** Arsenale **Meals** breakfast, dinner on request **Prices** LLLL	**Rooms** 1 bedroom (double or twin bed), living area with sofa-bed, kitchen, bathroom **Facilities** maid service, cook available **Credit cards** AE, DC, MC, V **Disabled** not suitable **Pets** not accepted **Closed** never **Proprietor** Marina Ferron

Dorsoduro

Town guest-house

La Galleria

Through an improbable entrance next to a craft gallery, from which this unpretentious little hotel takes its name, we climbed a flight of steepish steps and travelled back some 80 years, for La Galleria appears frozen in the Edwardian era. Dark red flock paper covers the walls; floors are mostly plain wooden boards; the furniture is traditional Venetian – silk and gilt bedheads, large old-fashioned beds and chandeliers; and there are few amenities. No. 10 is the room to go for. Right on the Grand Canal, it sleeps four, has a glorious painted ceiling and only costs L30,000 more than a standard double.

Nearby Accademia gallery; Grand Canal.

Accademia, Dorsoduro 878/a, 30123 Venezia **Tel** 041 5204172/5285814 **Fax** 041 5204172 **E-mail** galleria@tin.it **Location** at NE corner of Campo della Carità, next to the Accademia bridge; **vaporetto** Accademia or water taxi **Meals** breakfast, served in room **Prices** L	**Rooms** 10; 8 double and twin, 2 with bath; 1 single; 1 family with bath; all rooms have phone **Facilities** sitting area **Credit cards** not accepted **Disabled** not suitable **Pets** accepted **Closed** 2–3 weeks in winter **Proprietor** Luciano Benedetti

Restaurant-with-rooms

Locanda Montin

In the same family for generations, this *antica locanda* used to attract a devoted following among the glitteratti from Ezra Pound to Jimmy Carter. Fame was assured when the pergola-shaded garden became the setting for a scene in a film featuring Tony Musante and Florinda Bolkan, *Anonimo Veneziano*. Although it still has charisma, with paintings jostling for space on the walls, the restaurant is living off its reputation, serving ordinary food at highish prices. Bedrooms are basic, but lead off a magnificent beamed landing, furnished with ornate pieces and a wrought-iron chandelier.

Nearby Carmini; San Trovaso; Accademia gallery; Zattere.

San Trovaso, Fondamenta di Borgo, Dorsoduro 1147, Venezia **Tel** 041 5227151 **Fax** 041 5200255 **Location** just S of Calle Eremite; **vaporetto** Accademia, Ca' Rezzonico or water taxi **Meals** breakfast, lunch, dinner **Prices** L **Rooms** 8; 3 double and twin, 3	triple, 1 family, 3 with shower, 4 with basin; one single with basin **Facilities** sitting area, restaurant, garden **Credit cards** AE, DC, MC, V **Disabled** not suitable **Pets** accepted **Closed** 10 days Aug, 2–3 weeks Jan **Proprietor** Giuliamo Carretin

Cannaregio

Town hotel

Abbazia

If you haven't guessed its origins from the name, then the interior is sure to provide a clue. High-ceilinged corridors are peppered with doors to almost monastic bedrooms. The former abbey's refectory has been converted to a sitting room of vast proportions, with wood panelling, a stunning stone floor and perfectly preserved pulpit jutting out from one wall. Even the welcoming staff don't quite succeed in overcoming the feeling of austerity. We recommend bedrooms 302 and 303, both spacious with huge windows and walk-in cupboards. Best of all is the delightful mature garden.

Nearby station; Scalzi; Palazzo Labia; San Geremia.

Calle Priuli, Cannaregio 68, 30121 Venezia	triple and family, all with bath or shower; all rooms have phone, TV, air-conditioning, minibar, hairdrier
Tel 041 717333	
Fax 041 717949	
E-mail abbazia@iol.it	**Facilities** bar/sitting room, breakfast room, garden
Website www.venezialberghi.com	
Location just E of the station;	**Credit cards** AE, DC, MC, V
vaporetto Ferrovia	**Disabled** no special facilities
Meals breakfast	**Pets** not accepted
Prices LL	**Closed** never
Rooms 39 double and twin,	**Manager** Franco De Rossi

Town guest-house

Bernardi-Semenzato

Tucked away in a backstreet off the busy Strada Nova, this popular, reasonably priced hotel is handy for a visit to the church of Santi Apostoli, with its wonderful Tiepolo altarpiece. The Bernardi is a friendly, if eclectic place. Low beamed ceilings characterize the small ground floor, devoted to two breakfast rooms and dominated by a *trompe l'oeil* window, in which two children and a cat enjoy a fantasy view of Venice. Furnishings are modern and unfussy, bedrooms, modest; though one double room in a nearby annexe is decked out in a very different, over-the-top rococo style.

Nearby Ca' d'Oro; Santi Apostoli; Miracoli.

Calle dell' Oca, Santi Apostoli, Cannaregio 4366, 30121 Venezia	(1 in annexe), 10 with shower; 3 single; all rooms have phone, TV (on request), safe
Tel 041 5227257	
Fax 041 5222424	**Facilities** breakfast area and room
Location off NW corner of Campo Santi Apostoli;	**Credit cards** not accepted
vaporetto Ca' d'Oro	**Disabled** not suitable
Meals breakfast	**Pets** accepted
Prices L	**Closed** 2–3 weeks Jan
Rooms 16; 13 double and twin	**Proprietor** Leonardo Biasin

Lagoon Islands

Resort hotel, Giudecca

Cipriani

We have heard differing opinions about the world-famous Cipriani and its two suite annexes with butler service, Palazzo Vendramin and the new Palazzetto. Our own view is that it is astonishingly overpriced, but if you are happy to accept that, then you can relax and enjoy its principal assets: the peaceful location and fabulous pool. On the subject of which, one recent visitor told us: 'On a hot day we went for lunch, for which we were content to pay a great deal, then asked if our young daughter could swim in the deserted pool. We were told she could not – house rules. We returned gratefully to the Gritti.'

Nearby Il Redentore church; Venice; Lagoon Islands.

Giudecca 10, 30133 Venezia
Tel 041 5207744
Fax 041 5207745
E-mail info@hotelcipriani.it
Website www.orientexpresshotel.com
Location 5 mins from San Marco by launch; **vaporetto** 24-hr hotel launch
Meals breakfast, lunch, dinner
Prices LLLL
Rooms 99; 59 double and twin, 7 single, 33 suites, all with bath; all rooms have phone, TV, air-conditioning, hairdrier, safe
Facilities sitting rooms, dining rooms, bar, sauna, gym, lift, swimming pool, tennis court
Credit cards AE, DC, MC, V
Disabled access possible
Pets accepted
Closed never
Manager Natale Rusconi

Seafront hotel, Lido

Des Bains

Though strictly too large to qualify for this guide, the grand turn-of-the-century Des Bains is the best hotel on the Lido. With its flower-filled garden, swimming pool, dining terrace and private beach lined with bamboo huts, its facilities are unrivalled. Rooms are expensive but special offers can cut their cost by more than a third. Painted cream inside and out, its elegant, chandeliered, parquet-floored salons evoke memories for most visitors of the setting for Visconti's film version of *Death in Venice*, the novel Thomas Mann wrote here. Its refined Edwardian atmosphere has survived a takeover by the Sheraton chain.

Nearby Venice; Lagoon Islands.

Lungomare Marconi 17, Lido, 30126 Venezia **Tel** 041 5265921
Fax 041 5260113
E-mail RE078_DESBAINS@Sheraton.com
Website www.sheraton.com
Location on Adriatic coast, east of Gran Viale Santa Maria Elisabetta; **vaporetto** Lido
Meals breakfast, lunch, dinner
Prices LLLL **Rooms** 190; 157 double and twin, 14 single, 19 suites, all with bath; all rooms have phone, TV, air conditioning, minibar, hairdrier, safe
Facilities sitting rooms, dining room, bar, lift, terraces, garden, swimming pool, tennis court, beach **Credit cards** AE, DC, MC, V **Disabled** no special facilities **Pets** accepted
Closed Nov to mid-Mar
Manager Leone Jannuzzi

Lagoon Islands

Town hotel, Lido

La Meridiana

Although not right on the beach, La Meridiana has the sedate and quite agreeably old-fashioned air of a seaside hotel, which was purpose-built in the 1930s in rustic style, and where little seems to have changed since. Venetian marble floors and dark three-quarters panelled walls keep the ground floor refreshingly cool in summer. In winter, it has a more noticeably antiquated feel. In the main building, bedrooms are large and quite recently decorated. Numerous casement windows make them light and airy, and some have French doors on to a terrace. There are also nine rooms in a connecting annexe.

Nearby Venice; Lagoon Islands.

Via Lepanto 45, Lido, 30126 Venezia
Tel 041 5260343
Fax 041 5269240
E-mail info@lameridiana.com
Website www.lameridiana.com
Location at junction with Via Marcello; **vaporetto** San Nicolò
Meals breakfast
Prices LL
Rooms 34; 32 double and twin, with bath or shower; 2 single with shower; all rooms have phone, TV, air-conditioning, minibar, hairdrier, safe
Facilities sitting room, bar, breakfast room, lift, garden,
Credit cards AE, DC, MC, V
Disabled access possible
Pets accepted
Closed early Nov to Carnival
Proprietor Gianluca Regazzo

Town hotel, Lido

Villa Parco

Set back from the road, through wrought-iron gates, in a romantic, if overgrown garden full of poplars, oleanders and statuary, this 19thC villa still looks impressive despite its now peeling paint. The area is a quiet residential one, a few minutes' walk from the waterfront. The villa itself is in the art nouveau style, though furnishings are mainly modern. Airy bedrooms are 'clean and comfortable', according to a recent report which also commends the 'helpful staff'. Breakfast is served in a small room in the basement or, from May to September, under a canopy in the pretty garden.

Nearby Venice; Lagoon Islands.

Via Rodi 1, Lido, 30126 Venezia
Tel 041 5260015/5261495
Fax 041 5267620
Location at junction with Via Modone e Corone and Via D. Selvo; **vaporetto** San Nicolò
Meals breakfast, snacks
Prices LL
Rooms 22; 21 double and twin, triple and family, all with bath or shower; 1 single with shower; all rooms have phone, TV, air-conditioning, minibar
Facilities sitting area, breakfast room, garden, sun terrace, parking
Credit cards AE, DC, MC, V
Disabled not suitable
Pets accepted
Closed never
Manager Lea Zollino

Veneto

Town hotel, Asolo

Duse

The name was inspired by one of Asolo's best-known residents, the actress and mistress of D'Annunzio, Eleanor Duse. This cosy little hotel is decked out almost entirely in blue and yellow, with a spiral staircase and a tiny first-floor breakfast room. Dark wood furniture, striped curtains and blue bedspreads furnish all the bedrooms, with matching picture bows and fabric-covered lights, too twee for our taste. The best rooms are the doubles at the front, which include somewhere to sit, but pack your earplugs to block out the nearby Duomo's early matins bell. There has been a recent change of management here; we welcome reports.
Nearby Palladian villas; Possagno (10 km).

Via R. Browning 190,
31011 Asolo, Treviso
Tel 0423 55241
Fax 0423 950404
Location off SE corner of Piazza Maggiore; parking in Piazza Maggiore
Meals breakfast
Prices L
Rooms 14; 8 double and twin, all with bath; 5 single with shower; 1 suite with bath; all rooms have phone, TV, air-conditioning, minibar
Facilities breakfast room, lift
Credit cards AE, MC, V
Disabled access difficult
Pets accepted
Closed sometimes 2–3 weeks in Nov
Proprietor Elena de Checchi

Town hotel, Castelfranco Veneto

Al Moretto

Admirers of that enigmatic artist, Giorgione, will not want to by-pass Castelfranco Veneto, his birthplace. Within the moated Castello, its medieval core, you will find the Duomo and his *Madonna and Child* – flawed and damaged, yet magical.

Al Moretto, despite its modern appearance, is the oldest hostelry in town, in the same ownership for generations. Recently it was enlarged and refurbished, tastefully enough, but in a way that swaps character for streamlined comfort. You can be assured of a good night's rest in a well-equipped, softly coloured room, and a generous buffet breakfast.
Nearby Castello; Duomo; Casa del Giorgione.

Via San Pio X 10, 31033 Castelfranco Veneto, Treviso
Tel 0423 721313
Fax 0423 721066
E-mail albergo.al.moretto@apf.it
Website www.sevenonline.it/albergoalmoretto
Location outside the Castello, but in town centre, off Mercato on road to Asolo; parking
Meals breakfast
Prices L **Rooms** 34 single, double and twin, all with bath or shower; all rooms have phone, TV, air-conditioning, minibar, hairdrier, safe
Facilities sitting room, breakfast room, bar, lift, garden **Credit cards** AE, DC, MC, V **Disabled** access difficult **Pets** accepted
Closed never
Proprietor Signor Rigato

Veneto

Town inn, Cavaso del Tomba

Locanda Alla Posta

Cavaso del Tomba is a straggling village close to Possagno, birthplace of Canova and site of his moving Gipsoteca (gallery of plaster models) and his bizarre Temple. Alla Posta is a handsome building with something of the air of a Wild West saloon about it. There's a bar where locals congregate, and a simple restaurant in which surprisingly sophisticated food is served. Upstairs, wide, smartly decorated landings lead to the bedrooms, which are plain, but light, spacious and good value. Some are modern and functional, others – Nos 4 and 6 – have more interest, with matching Liberty furniture.

Nearby Possagno (2 km); Asolo (10 km).

Piazza XIII Martiri 13, 31034
Cavaso del Tomba, Treviso
Tel/Fax 0423 543112
Location in town centre, 6 km
W of SS348 at Pederobba
Meals breakfast, lunch, dinner
Prices L
Rooms 7; 5 double and twin, 2
family, all with shower; all
rooms have phone, TV
Facilities dining room, bar

Credit cards MC, V
Disabled not suitable
Pets accepted
Closed 1–15 July; restaurant
closed Tues, Wed eve
Proprietor Remo Visentin

Town hotel, Conegliano

Canon d'Oro

Standing above the Veneto plain, Conegliano is a commercial and industrial centre, and the birthplace of Cima, painter of radiant Venetian Renaissance altarpieces. Arcaded Via XX Settembre is lined with handsome mansions, one of which is this 16thC building. However, the hotel's frescoed exterior is the last you will see of the past: the interior is bland, with no original features and tired, functional public rooms. Bedrooms are better: Nos 305 and 306 under the eaves have most appeal. There is a flower-filled terraced garden, and despite its shortcomings, this is the best bet for a bed in Conegliano.

Nearby Treviso (28 km); Belluno (54 km).

Via XX Settembre 129, 31015
Conegliano, Treviso
Tel 0438 34246
Fax 0438 34246
E-mail canondoro@sevenonline.it
Website www.sevenonline.it/canondoro
Location in the heart of the old
town, with parking
Meals breakfast
Prices L
Rooms 35 double and twin and
single, 1 with bath, 34 with
shower; all rooms have phone,
TV, air-conditioning, minibar,
hairdrier
Facilities sitting room, breakfast
room, garden, lift
Credit cards AE, DC, MC, V
Disabled access difficult
Pets not accepted **Closed** never
Proprietors Giancarlo and
Piero Capraro

Veneto

Country villa, Dolo

Villa Ducale

When we visited this grand 19thC villa hotel, in a formal garden filled with statues, the marble-floored reception and vast chandeliered dining hall were seething with management consultants attending a reception. Not an uncommon event, since it has conference facilities for up to 200 people. Though recently restored, much of the original decoration looks dowdy, as it must have from the outset. Neutral colours predominate and, despite 19thC murals and decorative parquet floors, bedrooms have a shuttered-up feel. There is an apartment (No. 22) ideal for a family of five.

Nearby Palladian villas; Riviera del Brenta.

Riviera Martiri della Libertà 75, 30031 Dolo, Venezia **Tel/Fax** 041 5608020/5608004
Website www.villaducale.it
Location 2 km E of Dolo, on the SS11; in own grounds with ample parking
Meals breakfast, lunch, dinner
Prices L
Rooms 11; 6 double and twin, 3 triple, 2 family, all with bath or shower; all rooms have phone, TV, air-conditioning, minibar, hair-drier, safe **Facilities** breakfast room, sitting room, dining room, meeting room, bar, restaurant, garden **Credit cards** AE, DC, MC, V
Disabled ground-floor room
Pets accepted
Closed never
Manager Marco Fogarin

Country villa, Gorgo al Monticano

Villa Revedin

In open countryside just outside the little town of Gorgo al Monticano, Villa Revedin is sheltered within its own mature park. As the original structure of the 15thC villa remains intact, the mostly modern furnishings tend to jar – for instance, the bright chairs and contemporary mural in the classical entrance. Our inspector was impressed by the vast reading room with its marble floor and frescoed ceiling, but couldn't imagine curling up in here with a book. The rustic restaurant specializes in fish and looks as if it should be by the sea. As you go in, there's a long counter groaning with fresh fish on ice.

Nearby Treviso (32 km); Venice within reach.

Via Palazzi 4, Gorgo al Monticano, 31040 Oderzo, Treviso **Tel** 0422 800033
Fax 0422 800272
E-mail info@villarevedin.it
Website www.villarevedin.it
Location 4 km NE of Oderzo; in own grounds; parking
Meals breakfast, lunch, dinner
Prices L
Rooms 32; 14 double and twin, 14 single, 4 suites, all with bath or shower; all rooms have phone, TV, air-conditioning, minibar, hairdrier
Facilities breakfast room, sitting room, bar, restaurant
Credit cards AE, DC, MC, V
Disabled not suitable **Pets** not accepted **Closed** restaurant Sun dinner, Mon, Jan, 10 days Aug
Manager Stefano Bison

Veneto

Town hotel, Mogliano Veneto

Villa Stucky

In its own wood-fringed garden, Villa Stucky is an imposing 19thC building whose mid-European flavour can be traced to the Swiss Family Stucky who built it after demolishing a classical villa. Today it is favoured by business guests and conference organizers. The formality of the high-ceilinged public rooms is carried through to the bedrooms and suites, which have grandiose names – 'Principessa Sissi', 'Regina Margherita' – and decoration to match. Although under the old timbered roof, 'Estasi' and 'Venezia' are more modern in style. There's no shortage of space, even in standard doubles.

Nearby Venice (14 km); Treviso (10 km); Padua (30 km).

Via Don Bosco 47, 31021
Mogliano Veneto, Treviso
Tel 041 5904528
Fax 041 5904566
E-mail villastucky@stargas.it
Location in town centre; in grounds with parking
Meals breakfast, lunch, dinner
Prices LL
Rooms 20; 11 double and twin, 5 single, 4 junior suites all with bath or shower; all rooms have phone, TV, fax/modem point, air-conditioning, minibar, hairdrier, safe
Facilities sitting area, dining room, bar, lift, garden **Credit cards** AE, DC, MC, V
Disabled no special facilities
Pets not accepted
Closed 2 weeks in Aug
Manager Antonio Pianura

Restaurant-with-rooms, Montagnana

Aldo Moro

Montagnana is one of the most attractive towns in the Veneto, its arcaded streets enclosed by a superb rectangle of moated medieval walls. The Aldo Moro, opened in 1940 by the present owner's father (not the assassinated politician) makes the best base for an overnight stay. Bedrooms are a rather jarring mix of old and new, featuring glossy black headboards and wardrobes, and in each, a startlingly bright red armchair. Some bathrooms are large, with inviting showers properly enclosed. The restaurant rambles over several rooms, gleaming with polished glass and carefully folded napery.

Nearby Villa Pisani; Este (15 km); Padua (49 km).

Via Marconi 27, 35044
Montagnana, Padova
Tel 0429 81351
Fax 0429 82842
Location in town centre; parking in hotel garage or in street
Meals breakfast, lunch, dinner
Prices L
Rooms 25; 20 double and twin, 5 suites, all with shower; all rooms have phone, TV, air-conditioning; minibar in suites
Facilities restaurant, breakfast room, sitting area, bar, meeting room, small garden **Credit cards** AE, DC, MC, V
Disabled not suitable
Pets accepted **Closed** 2 weeks in Jan, 2 weeks in Aug; restaurant closed Mon
Proprietor Sergio Moro

Veneto

Town hotel, Padua

Leon Bianco

'Charming' may not be quite the right word for this modern hotel, with its plate-glass doors and smooth contemporary furnishings. But it has a certain – if somewhat self-conscious – style, and a great position overlooking the famous Caffè Pedrocchi. To be avoided by the prudish though – a screen decorated with an explicit nude mural dominates the small green sitting room. Bedrooms are remarkably large with parquet floors, white formica furniture and framed American posters. Summer guests are served breakfast beneath calico parasols on a roof terrace lined with plants in terracotta pots.

Nearby Palazzo della Ragione; Scrovegni Chapel; Il Santo.

Piazzetta Pedrocchi 12, 35122 Padova
Tel 049 8750814
Fax 049 8756184
E-mail leonbianco@toscanelli.com
Website www.toscanelli.com
Location opposite Caffè Pedrocchi, just E of Piazza delle Erbe; garage parking
Meals breakfast
Prices L

Rooms 22; 20 double and twin, triple and family, 4 with bath, 16 with shower; 2 single with shower; all rooms have phone, TV, air-conditioning, minibar
Facilities breakfast room, sitting area, lift, roof terrace
Credit cards AE, DC, MC, V
Disabled access difficult
Pets accepted **Closed** never
Manager Paulo Morosi

Town hotel, Padua

Majestic Toscanelli

The hotel is neither majestic nor Tuscan but it does occupy an unusually quiet spot in the heart of old Padua, with a welcome splash of flowers and greenery in the little square outside. Though the Toscanelli has long appeared in our all-Italy guide, a night's stay persuaded us that it was nothing very special, and we were somewhat baffled to know why it was classed as a four star. Bedrooms, whether described as 'Venetian', 'Louis-Philippe' or '19thC English', are run-of-the-mill. Recent changes include a new reception desk and lobby with a balcony, a breakfast lounge, and improvements to the showers. Reports, please.

Nearby Palazzo della Ragione; Scrovegni Chapel; Il Santo.

Via dell' Arco 2, 35122 Padova
Tel 049 663244
Fax 049 8760025
E-mail majestic@toscanelli.com
Website www.toscanelli.com
Location town centre, near Piazza delle Erbe; by car follow signs for Zona Sud, then pick up helpful hotel signs; parking
Meals breakfast **Prices** LL
Rooms 32; 26 double and twin,

3 superior double and twin; 3 suites, all with bath or shower; all rooms have phone, TV, air-conditioning, minibar, hairdrier; safe in some rooms
Facilities breakfast room, sitting room, bar, lift **Credit cards** AE, DC, MC, V **Disabled** access possible **Pets** accepted **Closed** never
Proprietor Anna-Maria Morosi

Veneto

Azienda Agrituristica, Pozzolo

Valle Verde

In a lush, peaceful valley, this cream-painted house offers five modest bedrooms with modern facilities, but its *raison d'être* is a bustling restaurant with a vast terrace for *al fresco* meals. There is no menu, but *mamma* – Evelina – does all the cooking herself, producing what she feels like and does best: pasta, roast meat – simple country fare. The restaurant is furnished with rush-seated chairs; immaculate linen covers the tables. Huge arched glass doors open on to the terrace, beyond which is a playground where children can slide and swing amidst the vines. This *agriturismo* is a cut above the norm.

Nearby Palladian villas; Vicenza (24 km).

Via Fagnini 13, 36020 Pozzolo di Villaga, Vicenza
Tel 0444 868586
Location from Arcugnano, take right turn to Barbarano, signed Pozzolo, then keep left for Valverde; ample parking
Meals breakfast, lunch, dinner
Prices L
Rooms 5; 1 twin, 1 triple, 2 family, all with shower; 1 single with bath; all rooms have phone, TV (on request)
Facilities restaurant, garden
Credit cards not accepted
Disabled access difficult
Pets not accepted
Closed restaurant Mon
Proprietors Donello family

Chalet guest-house, Tai di Cadore

Villa Marinotti

Tai di Cadore lies just along the road from Pieve di Cadore, birthplace of Titian and the main town in this mountainous and thickly wooded region, and Villa Marinotti has a typical back-drop of dark forest and rocky peaks.

The owners of the modern stone, wood and white-painted chalet, open only in summer, have created five spacious and comfortable suites, each one with its own little sitting room, sleeping up to four people, and recently, two one-bedroomed chalets. There is a dining room serving good home cooking, and in the expansive grounds are a sauna and tennis court.

Nearby Pieve di Cadore (1.5 km); Cortina d'Ampezzo (30 km).

Via Manzago 21, 32040 Tai di Cadore, Belluno
Tel 0435 32231
Fax 0435 33335
E-mail villa.marinotti@libero.it
Website www.villa-marinotti.itgo.com
Location in village, on SS51 Cortina to Pieve di Cadore road (1.5 km SE of Pieve); ample parking
Meals breakfast, dinner
Prices L
Rooms 5 suites, 2 chalets, all with bath; all rooms have phone, TV **Facilities** sitting room, dining room, bar, meeting room, terrace **Credit cards** AE, MC, V **Disabled** access difficult **Pets** not accepted
Closed Oct to Jun
Proprietors Laura and Giorgio Marinotti

Veneto

Country hotel, Torri del Benaco

Europa

The decoration in this 1950s villa is typical of the period: brown colour schemes, modern wood panelling, garish floor tiles. However, the friendly Casarottis have done their best to knock off some of the hard edges with fresh flowers, and to make what regular visitors call 'a happy, welcoming hotel'. Bright rugs rescue the sitting room from being too gloomy, and the dining room is airy and light, if a trifle banal. Bedrooms look more up-to-date, with colourful fabrics; seven have views of Lake Garda. The setting is pleasant and the pretty garden includes a shady terrace for breakfast or candlelit dinners.

Nearby Sirmione (38 km); Verona (45 km).

Via G. D'Annunzio 13–15, 37010 Torri del Benaco, Verona
Tel 045 7225086
Fax 045 6296632
E-mail hoteleuropa@garda-access.com
Location 150 m off main Gardesana road, just S of town; in own grounds with ample parking **Meals** breakfast, lunch, dinner **Prices** L

Rooms 18; 17 double and twin, 7 with bath, 8 with shower; 1 single; all rooms have phone, hairdrier
Facilities sitting room, bar, dining room, garden, swimming pool **Credit cards** MC, V **Disabled** no special facilities **Pets** not accepted
Closed mid-Oct to Easter
Proprietors Casarotti family

Restaurant-with-rooms, Treviso

Alle Beccherie/Campeol

Alle Beccherie is an unpretentious family-run restaurant at the heart of old Treviso. 'Superb food without being overpriced,' says one recent visitor, while others praise the dignified, old-fashioned atmosphere of this fine old Venetian-style building. Across the street is the owner's Albergo Campeol, which has mostly large, plain rooms with big beds and modern furnishings, including roomy wardrobes. Our bathroom had a huge shower and cruelly effective mirror lighting, and the spacious bedroom had a canal view. Be prepared for a gruff and peremptory welcome from the non English-speaking *patron*.

Nearby Piazza dei Signori; Palazzo dei Trecento; Duomo.

Piazza Ancilotto 10, 31100 Treviso
Tel 0422 540871/56601
Fax 0422 540871
Location city centre; parking in street, or in car park in Piazza del Duomo
Meals breakfast, lunch, dinner
Prices L
Rooms 14 single, double and twin, all with shower; all rooms

have phone, TV, hairdrier
Facilities dining room, breakfast room
Credit cards AE, DC, MC, V
Disabled not suitable
Closed restaurant closed Sun eve, Mon, Aug
Proprietor Signor Campeol

Veneto

Agriturismo, Valdobbiadene

Riva de Milàn

As we were shown around this ranch-style *agriturismo* by Signora Bernardi, an elderly woman who only speaks Italian, we were struck by how rustic this place is. Although the locality is almost suburban, the cream house with wooden shutters and doors and a large veranda is on a working farm, where they breed peacocks as a sideline. As you'd expect, the cheerful restaurant offers morning-fresh produce and home cooking. Six simple rooms in contemporary country style nestle at the top of the house under a sloping beamed roof, with modern wood furniture and brand-new showers.

Nearby Asolo (26 km); Belluno (47 km); Treviso (36 km).

Via Erizzo 126, Valdobbiadene, Treviso
Tel 0423 973496/973030
Location from Valdobbiadene, off road to Bigolino, past sign to Villa Nova and up unmarked track to right through vines; ample parking
Meals breakfast, lunch, dinner
Prices L
Rooms 6 double and twin, all with shower; all rooms have TV
Facilities restaurant
Credit cards not accepted
Disabled access difficult
Pets accepted
Closed restaurant Sep to Easter and Mon
Proprietors Bernardi family

Agriturismo, Villorba

Podere del Convento

Podere del Convento is a working farm producing wine and fruit, an equestrian centre and a restaurant, with six attractive bedrooms also available. These have roughcast walls and ceilings open to the tiled roof, with large beds in bright yellow or peach, prettily upholstered bedroom chairs and the odd attractive piece of old country furniture. Bathrooms are tiled in primary colours.

The rambling, busily decorated restaurant is homely and bustling, often packed with local families. No English is spoken. by the Miliani family.

Nearby Palladian villas; Treviso (5 km); Venice (40 km).

Via 1V Novembre 16, 31050 Villorba, Treviso
Tel 0422 920044
Fax 0422 608403
Location in Villorba, off the SS13, 5 km N of Treviso, set amid farmland
Meals breakfast, lunch, dinner
Prices L
Rooms 6 double, all with shower; all rooms have phone
Facilities dining room, bar; riding available
Credit cards AE, MC, V
Children accepted
Disabled not suitable
Pets not accepted
Closed Aug
Proprietor Renzo Milani

Lombardia

Lakeside hotel, Limone sul Garda

Capo Reamol

Lake Garda is famous for its winds, and this relaxed and comfortable hotel (standing on a particularly breezy spot), provides some of the best facilities around, including a beefy German windsurfing instructor. Though the hotel lacks character, the unremarkable building enjoys a marvellous setting, with the bar and restaurant situated by the lake, and the activities on offer are numerous. The health and beauty team will try to eliminate your stress, or you could go for a punishing (or gentle) mountain bike ride. In the evening, you might find yourself dressing up in a toga for one of the hotel's regular Roman feasts.
Nearby Riva del Garda and ferries (11 km); Gardone (30 km).

25010 Limone sul Garda, Brescia
Tel 0365 954040
Fax 0365 954262
E-mail hcreamol@anthesi.com
Location just N of town on lakeside; in own grounds with ample parking **Meals** breakfast, lunch, dinner **Prices** L
Rooms 59; 56 double and twin, 3 with bath, 53 with shower; 3 single with shower; all rooms have phone, TV, minibar, hairdrier
Facilities restaurant, bar, sauna, fitness/beauty centre, terraces, swimming pool, beach
Credit cards not accepted
Disabled specially adapted rooms available **Pets** not accepted **Closed** mid-Oct to May **Proprietor** Angelica Glas

Lakeside villa, Sirmione

Villa Cortine Palace

The setting of this luxury headland hotel, a many-columned neoclassical villa, is memorable. From the charming streets of Sirmione, vast iron gates admit you to a private drive which sweeps past elaborate fountains and statues set in magnificent exotic gardens. Inside the late-19thC villa are a series of frescoed and highly ornamented public rooms and five elegant bedrooms. The rest of the suitably well-appointed bedrooms, all with lake-facing balconies, are in the grim 1950s extension, which is as banal as the villa is grandiose. To sum up: hardly charming and small, but special, with unmissable grounds.
Nearby Lake Garda; Brescia (39 km); Verona (35 km).

Via Grotte 6, 25019 Sirmione, Brescia **Tel** 030 9905890
Fax 030 916390
E-mail info@hotelvillacortine.com
Website www.hotelvillacortine.com
Location 1 km beyond Sirmione; ample parking
Meals breakfast, lunch, dinner
Prices LLLL; half board obligatory in high season
Rooms 49; 43 twin, 2 suites, 4 junior suites, all with bath; all rooms have phone, TV, airconditioning, minibar, hairdrier **Facilities** sitting rooms, dining rooms, bar, lift, gardens, terraces, swimming pool, tennis court, private beach **Credit cards** AE, DC, MC, V **Disabled** no special facilities **Pets** accepted **Closed** Nov to Apr **Manager** Roberto Cappelletto

Trentino-Alto Adige

Country hotel, Alberé di Tenna

Margherita

In a pine forest on a mountainside, this family-run hotel could hardly have a more peaceful setting. Although peace is of the essence (a sign requests you to avoid 'unnecessary noise'), families are positively encouraged. One swimming pool is specifically for children, with a playground reassuringly close to the sun-loungers, and two spacious apartments are ideal for families. A modern chalet, it has a lovely big terrace at the front, but uninspired decoration inside. Public rooms are airy but characterless. The original 1950s bedrooms tend to be small and dreary, so ask for one of the larger new rooms.

Nearby Trento (21 km); Lago di Caldonazzo (5 km).

kLocalità Pineta Alberé 2, 38050 Tenna, Trento
Tel 0461 706445/706045
Fax 0461 707854
Location NE of Tenna; in own grounds with ample parking
Meals breakfast, lunch, dinner
Prices L
Rooms 52; 41 double and twin, 8 single, 3 family, all with bath or shower; all rooms have phone, TV, hairdrier **Facilities** sitting/games room, dining room, meeting room, bar, garden, swimming pool, tennis court
Credit cards AE, MC, V
Children welcome
Disabled no special facilities
Pets accepted
Closed Nov to Feb
Proprietor Lino Angeli

Country castle, Appiano Monte

Schloss Freudenstein

Set amidst vines and fruit trees, this 800-year-old castle enjoys wonderful views. The building is imposing, rather sombre and beginning to crumble ... but not without atmosphere. There is a romantic inner courtyard, with stone arches and ancient uneven flagstones, and you can dine on the *loggia* which runs alongside. Beyond, amongst a series of rather ghostly rooms, a vast frescoed hall acts as the sitting room, and there is a cosier bar. Bedrooms are either large or huge, comfortable but lacking in style. Our set-menu dinner was elegantly presented by the gracious proprietor. More guest house than hotel.

Nearby Bolzano (10 km); Lake Caldaro (10 km).

Via Masaccio 6, Appiano Monte 39057 Bolzano
Tel 0471 660638
Fax 0471 660122
Location 10 km SW of Bolzano, in own grounds with ample parking
Meals breakfast, dinner
Prices L-LL
Rooms 14 single, double and twin and family rooms, all with bath or shower; all rooms have phone, hairdrier, safe
Facilities dining room, sitting room, courtyard, bar, garden, swimming pool **Credit cards** not accepted **Children** accepted
Disabled not suitable
Pets not accepted
Closed mid-Nov to mid-Mar
Proprietor Gisela Ehmer-Insam

Trentino-Alto Adige

Town hotel, Castelrotto

Cavallino d'Oro

Records of this former coaching inn date back to 1393. Located on the central square of postcard-pretty Castelrotto, the hotel has a pleasant, professional and energetic host in Stefan Urthaler, whose family have been in charge for three generations.

Parts are ancient and charming, particularly two of the dining rooms and the bar, popular with schnapps-swilling locals. Other public areas lack character, and bedrooms facing the church walls are gloomy, with banal lighting. Ask for one of the much preferable wood-panelled rooms.

Nearby Alpe ade Siusi; Val Gardena.

Piazza Kraus, 39040 Castelrotto, Bolzano
Tel 0471 706337
Fax 0471 707172
E-mail cavallino@cavallino.it
Website www.cavallino.it
Location in town centre, 24 km NE of Bolzano; ample parking
Meals breakfast, lunch, dinner
Prices LL
Rooms 22; 17 double and twin, 2 single, 3 suites, all with bath; all rooms have phone, TV, hairdrier, safe
Facilities dining rooms, bar, sauna, solarium
Credit cards AE, DC, MC, V
Disabled access difficult
Pets accepted
Closed mid-Nov to mid-Dec
Proprietors Stefan and Susanne Urthaler

Country hotel, Cognola di Trento

Villa Madruzzo

This is an imposing, red and yellow villa in neoclassical style, well placed for visiting Trento and set in lovely gardens – it is a shame that traffic noise from the nearby main road permeates the peace. Public rooms are pleasant, particularly the three dining rooms which are decorated along elegant, classical lines with Venetian chandeliers and a few well-placed antique sideboards and portraits. The spacious terrace running along two sides of the house provides plenty of room for outdoor eating. Bedrooms in the main villa have more character than those in the rather banal extension.

Nearby Trento; Valsugana (10 km); Lake Caldonazzo (10 km).

Via Ponte Alto 26, 38050 Cognola di Trento, Trento
Tel 0461 986220
Fax 0461 986361
E-mail info@villamadruzzo.it
Location 3 km NE of Trento; in grounds with parking
Meals breakfast, lunch, dinner
Prices L
Rooms 51; 26 double and twin, 22 single, 3 triple, 4 with bath, 47 with shower; all rooms have phone, TV, minibar, hairdrier, safe
Facilities restaurant, bar, lift, terraces, garden
Credit cards AE, DC, MC, V
Disabled ramps to public rooms, bedrooms on ground floor, wide lift **Pets** accepted
Closed restaurant Sun
Proprietor Signor Polonioli

Trentino-Alto Adige

Mountain chalet, Colfosco

Cappella

The present owners are the fourth generation to manage the hotel, which was rebuilt in classic chalet style in the 1960s. Renata Pizzinini's grandfather, a famous guide who collected walkers from Brunico by horse, pioneered tourism in the area. The hotel is comfortable and welcoming, but a trifle cluttered and fabrics are over-patterned. Tables are packed into the dining room, and myriad burnished metal lights are suspended from the ornate panelled ceiling. You can enjoy an indoor pool, skiing or walking from the door and spectacular views. There are 17 rooms in the Tyrolean-style Residence next door.

Nearby Brunico (34 km); Corvara (3 km); Cortina (36 km).

39030 Colfosco, Bolzano
Tel 0471 836183
Fax 0471 836561
E-mail cappella@altabadia.it
Website www.altabadia.it/cappella
Location on edge of village, W of Corvara; in garden; parking
Meals breakfast, lunch, dinner
Prices LL **Rooms** 40; 30 double and twin, 6 single, 2 with bath, 4 with shower; 4 suites, all with bath or shower; all rooms have phone, TV, minibar (on request), safe **Facilities** sitting room, bar, dining room, indoor swimming pool, sauna, solarium, gym, lift, terrace **Credit cards** AE, DC, MC, V **Disabled** no special facilities **Pets** accepted **Closed** Oct to mid-Dec, Apr to mid-June **Proprietor** Renata Pizzinini

Resort hotel, Corvara

La Perla

We include the four-star La Perla for those who are looking for a touch of luxury and plenty of facilities in their Dolomite hotel without losing too much character. Situated in the centre of Corvara, in the heart of the lovely Alpine region of Alta Badia, the hotel is extremely comfortable in 'sophisticated rustic' style and offers an indoor spa with heated pool, whirlpool, turkish bath, sauna, solarium and massage, as well as an outdoor heated pool for summer. The restaurant, La Stuä de Michil, serves elegant dishes. The modern bedrooms lack the character of the many public rooms, but are well equipped.

Nearby Val Gardena; Cortina d'Ampezzo (36 km).

Via Centro 44, 39033 Corvara in Badia, Bolzano
Tel 0471 836133
Fax 0471 836568
E-mail perla@altabadia.it
Website www.altabadia.it/laperla
Location in town centre; ample parking **Meals** breakfast, lunch, dinner **Prices** LLLL
Rooms 52 double and twin, single and suites, all with bath; all rooms have phone, TV, hairdrier **Facilities** sitting rooms, dining rooms, games room, lift, terrace, indoor and outdoor swimming pool **Credit cards** AE, DC, MC, V **Disabled** access possible **Pets** accepted **Closed** mid-Dec to mid-Apr, July to Sep **Proprietors** Costa family

Trentino-Alto Adige

Country apartments, Fié allo Sciliar

Moarhof

This is an area where it is easy to find simple accommodation: every other house offers rooms or apartments for rent. This 12thC farmhouse building with a sundial painted on the front caught our eye as being special. Situated just above the village of Fié, there are eight apartments for between two and five people, and all are decorated in rustic Tyrolean farmhouse style. Several boast their original wood panelling and ceramic stoves; most have separate sitting and bedrooms, and well-equipped kitchen areas (with washing machine and dishwasher). There are two with balconies.

Nearby Bolzano (20 km); Castelrotto (10 km).

39050 Fié allo Sciliar, Bolzano
Tel/Fax 0471 725095
Location 20 km E of Bolzano, outside village; in own garden with ample parking
Meals none
Prices L
Rooms 8 apartments; all apartments have kitchen, bathroom, TV (on request)
Facilities table tennis, garden, swimming pool, barbecue
Credit cards not accepted
Disabled not suitable
Pets accepted
Closed never
Proprietors Kompatscher family

Mountain hotel, La Villa

La Villa

If you want to stay in the lovely Alta Badia region of the Dolomites, here is a simpler alternative to La Perla in Corvara (see page 158). Unfortunately we were unable to send an inspector as the hotel was closed at the time, but we include it on the strength of a letter of recommendation, which praises its beautiful and peaceful setting on the slope of a hillside with wide views across the valley. 'An old mountain building completely renovated, with a garden full of flowers in summer. Inside the hotel is fresh and neat, with lots of white walls, natural fabrics and modern pine furniture.'

Nearby Corvara (4.5 km); Cortina d'Ampezzo (35 km).

La Villa, 39030 Alta Badia, Bolzano
Tel 0471 847035
Fax 0471 847393
E-mail lavilla@altabadia.it
Website www.altabadia.it/hotellavilla
Location off SS244 Corvara to Brunico road, 4.5 km N of Corvara; with parking
Meals breakfast, lunch, dinner
Prices L-LL
Rooms 27 double, twin and single, all with bath or shower; all rooms have phone, TV, hairdrier **Facilities** sitting room, dining room, lift, sauna/fitness room terrace **Credit cards** MC, V **Disabled** access difficult
Pets not accepted
Closed mid-Apr to mid-June and mid-Sep to Dec
Manager Mariangela Pizzinini

Trentino-Alto Adige

Medieval manor, Merano

Castel Rundegg

A recent reporter wrote about this hotel, '... a lovely old building, but it's a pity it doesn't enjoy a more rural setting. It's on quite a busy road with other buildings close by.' She found Castel Rundegg, 'a bit too slick and very beauty farm orientated'. The health and beauty complex is certainly impressive, and guests can submit themselves to all the latest treatments. The restaurant has a gothic stone-vaulted ceiling and alcove rooms. Bedrooms are well-appointed with luxurious bathrooms and special features. One of the most sought-after, the turret room, commands a 360-degree view.

Nearby Passirio river; Adige valley; Passirio valley.

Via Scena 2, 39012 Merano, Bolzano **Tel** 0473 234100 **Fax** 0473 237200 **Location** on E side of Merano; in own grounds with ample parking **Meals** breakfast, lunch, dinner **Prices** L-LL **Rooms** 30; 22 double and twin, 20 with bath, 2 with shower; 5 single with shower; 1 suite, 1 family, both with bath; all rooms have phone, TV, minibar, hairdrier, safe **Facilities** sitting room, bar, dining rooms, indoor swimming pool, sauna, health and beauty farm, lift, garden **Credit cards** AE, DC, MC, V **Children** accepted **Disabled** not suitable **Pets** accepted **Closed** never **Proprietors** Sinn family

Mountain guest-house, San Cipriano

Stefaner

High up in the beautiful Tires valley, this is a fairly new Tyrolean chalet whose wooden balconies are a riot of colour in summer (unfortunately views from the front are interrupted by a row of lofty trees). Inside, furnishings are modern and uniform, and the carpet is busily patterned, but warm colours and a roaring fire in cold weather impart a cosy atmosphere. The simply-furnished rooms all have balconies and, though some are small, are spotless. The young Villgrattners are warm hosts, and Giorgio is an excellent and creative cook – dinner is served on the stroke of seven. Great value for money.

Nearby Bolzano (17 km); Sciliar Natural Park (2 km); skiing.

San Cipriano, 39050 Tires, Bolzano **Tel** 0471 642175 **Fax** 0471 642302 **E-mail** stefaner@rolmail.net **Website** www.stefaner.com **Location** on main road in village, 17 km E of Bolzano, 3 km E of Tires; with parking **Meals** breakfast, dinner **Prices** L **Rooms** 16; 14 double and twin, 2 with bath, 12 with shower; 2 single with shower; all rooms have phone, TV on request **Facilities** sitting room, dining room, bar, lift, garden **Credit cards** not accepted **Disabled** access possible **Pets** not accepted **Closed** 5 Nov to 26 Dec, mid-Jan to Feb **Proprietors** Villgrattner family

Trentino-Alto Adige

Mountain guest-house, San Floriano

Obereggen

The setting for this modest chalet is ideal for skiers. At the top of a gorgeous Dolomite valley, 1,550 metres above sea level, it is only yards from lifts which give access to 40 kilometres of piste (one in use during summer). From the sunny terrace you can watch nearby sporting activity or the sun setting behind craggy peaks across the valley. The focal point of the hotel is the cosy bar with its ceramic stove, stags' heads and hunting trophies. The bedrooms are simple but clean with plump duvets adding a touch of comfort. About half have balconies, and those at the top enjoy fabulous views. Charming hostess; good food.
Nearby Bolzano (15 km); skiing at Latemar ski centre.

Via Obereggen 8, San Floriano (Obereggen), 39050 Nova Ponente, Bolzano
Tel 0471 615572
Fax 0471 615889
Location 17 km SE of Bolzano Nord motorway exit, 5 km off SS241; on edge of village with parking
Meals breakfast, dinner
Prices L

Rooms 12; 11 double (2 twin), 1 single, all with shower; all rooms have phone
Credit cards not accepted
Disabled access difficult
Pets accepted
Closed after Easter to June, mid-Oct to Dec
Proprietors Pichler family

Mountain chalet, Selva

Sporthotel Granvara

The name says it all. Facilities include a squash court, gym and indoor pool. For ski enthusiasts, it offers direct access to the Sella Ronda and the Dolomite superski area via the Ciampinoi cable car, and at the end of the day, you can ski back to the door. If you need advice, the owner and his son are both instructors. Like many hotels in the area, it is a chalet, surrounded by pastures and glorious scenery, its wooden balconies brimming with geraniums in summer. Inside, the large comfortable Tyrolean-style public rooms are particularly inviting after a hard day on the slopes. Bedrooms are relatively anonymous.
Nearby Bolzano (40 km); Bressanone (35 km).

39048 Selva Gardena, Bolzano
Tel 0471 795250
Fax 0471 794336
E-mail granvara@gardena.net
Website www.granvara.com
Location 1 km E of Selva; in garden with parking and garage
Meals breakfast, lunch, dinner
Prices L
Rooms 32; 20 double and twin, 2 single, 10 suites, all with bath

or shower; all rooms have phone, TV, hairdrier, safe
Facilities sitting rooms, bar, dining room, conference room, indoor pool, sauna, squash court, gym, lift, garden **Credit cards** AE, MC, V **Disabled** no special facilities **Pets** not accepted **Closed** late Apr to mid-June, mid-Oct to early Dec
Proprietors Senoner family

Trentino-Alto Adige

Mountain hotel, Sesto

Tirol

The little town of Sesto (or Sexten) is one of the prettiest in the region, and the surrounding area must be one of the most beautiful parts of the Dolomites. The Berghotel Tirol is a recently constructed chalet, with dark wood balconies overlooking classic alpine scenery: a gentle valley dotted with chalets, a church spire in the foreground, and in the distance, the jagged peaks which are so characteristic of the area. In summer, there are walking trails; in winter you can ski. The comfortable, pine-furnished hotel is run with great hospitality and efficiency by the Holzer family. For self-caterers, there is an apartment-house next door.
Nearby Cortina d'Ampezzo (44 km).

Moso, 39030 Sesto, Bolzano
Tel 0474 710386
Fax 0474 710455
E-mail info@berghotel.com
Website www.berghotel.com
Location in Moso, 2 km SE of Sesto, which is on the SS355, 44 km NE of Cortina; ample parking **Meals** breakfast, lunch, dinner **Prices** L
Rooms 45 double and twin, single and suites, all with bath or shower; all rooms have phone, TV, hairdrier
Facilities sitting room, dining room, bar, sauna/solarium, lift, terrace
Credit cards not accepted
Disabled access difficult
Pets accepted **Closed** Easter to mid-May, Oct to Christmas
Proprietors Holzer family

Castle restaurant-with-rooms, Tirolo

Schloss Thurnstein

You must negotiate 4 kilometres of tortuous hairpin bends to reach this grey stone edifice built in 1200 as a defence tower for nearby Castel Tirolo. The reputation of the restaurant is well-established, and chef Toni Bauer is a larger-than-life figure, passionate about unpretentious cooking using the freshest of ingredients. Activity revolves around the series of dining rooms, and the two terraces (one on each side of the building – ideal for juggling sun and shade) have spectacular views. The comfortable bedrooms are in a nearby annexe; some have separate sitting areas.
Nearby Merano (5 km); Bolzano (28 km); Castel Tirolo (2 km).

Tirolo, 39019 Merano, Bolzano
Tel 0473 220255
Fax 0473 220558
Location 5 km N of Merano on mountainside with limited parking
Meals breakfast, lunch, dinner
Prices L
Rooms 10; 8 double (one twin), 2 single, all with bath or shower; all rooms have phone
Facilities restaurants, terraces, sitting room
Credit cards MC, V
Disabled not suitable
Pets not accepted
Closed early to mid-July, mid-Nov to mid-Mar
Proprietors Bauer family

Trentino-Alto Adige

Mountain restaurant-with-rooms, Villandro

Ansitz Zum Steinbock

Villandro is a pretty mountain village, and Ansitz Zum Steinbock stands at its centre. An imposing 18thC building, it looks rather forbidding from the outside, but the jolly terrace (where you can eat in warm weather) is a clue to the welcoming, typically Tyrolean interior – fresh and simple, with pine-clad or white-painted walls, pretty fabrics for curtains and tablecloths and rustic furniture and artefacts here and there. You will eat well: the restaurant is highly regarded locally for its regional cooking. Bedrooms are beamed, with modern pine beds and plump white duvets.

Nearby Bressanone (13 km); Val Gardena; Bolzano (28 km).

San Stefano 38, 39040
Villandro, Bolzano
Tel 0472 843111
Fax 0472 843468
E-mail steinbock@dnet.it
Location off SS12, Chiusa exit, 28 km NE of Bolzano; in village with parking
Meals breakfast, lunch, dinner
Prices L
Rooms 15 double and twin, 1 single, all with bath or shower; all rooms have phone, TV
Facilities dining rooms, terrace
Credit cards AE, MC, V
Disabled access difficult
Pets accepted
Closed mid-Jan to mid-Mar; restaurant Mon
Proprietors Signor and Signora Kirchbaumer

The Orient Express

The Venice-Simplon Orient Express

A journey on the Orient Express has many of the qualities of a stay in a charming small hotel - and much else besides. It is the most enchanting way of all to travel to Venice - at a price. Fiona and Andrew Duncan decided to find out just what you can expect for your money.

It was not a good start. As we were directed to a position at the overcrowded Orient Express check-in desk at London's Victoria Station, we were roundly abused and accused of queue-barging by a fellow-passenger. One or two others sprang to our defence. There was nearly an ugly scene. Perhaps there would be a murder on this Orient Express.

In the mock-'twenties waiting room we surveyed our companions. Many of the occupants seemed a great deal older than the period armchairs, each with an antimacassar, in which they sat. Others were younger, but scored low on glamour. One was videoing the empty chair opposite. Then a vision appeared - a blonde beauty clutching an Asprey carrier bag and a much older husband. This, surely, was our *femme fatale*, the bit of glamour they absolutely promised us on the Orient Express.

We felt a mite dispirited.... until the British Pullman which was to take us as far as Folkstone pulled into the platform. It was a gorgeous sight, each curtained window framing a white-clothed table, a red-shaded lamp, a vase of freesias. We boarded, and were instantly soothed, cheered by the champagne lunch and the cosy intimacy of our carriage as we chuntered through the dreary suburbs. We were in Ibis, built in 1925, with Greek dancing girls decorating the marquetry panels.

We will pass over the crossing to France. Enough to say that, as yet, there is no Orient Express-style equivalent to the Sea Cat, although the charming hostesses do their best with unwanted boxes of wine and snacks and encouraging smiles. We were in a separate seating area, cordoned off from ordinary mortals. We felt rather embarassed, and would have much preferred to sit with everyone else. "Ooh look," people pointed, "those are the nobs from the Orient Express."

And so to the continental train, the Orient Express itself. We squeezed along the corridor of our carriage to our little compartment (they are all the same size, with a communicating door for those who wish to take two together). How exquisite it was, with its banquette seat, its little table, its washbasin with cupboards and shelves tucked behind curved doors, its large window. How kind and helpful our steward, and how lovely to be alone. We made ourselves at home, then later ventured to the piano-bar, but finding it stuffed with a gaudy group of champagne-swilling, flash-bulb popping smokers, we hastily retreated. We ordered drinks, and emerged again only for dinner, when the darkening skies, intimate lighting and ravishing dining cars managed to flatter almost everyone. There was our *femme fatale*, resplendent in evening gown, her husband, like many others, in black tie. After dinner, as the train hurtled through the night, our companions packed into the piano bar. Wobbling and jiggling in their seats, liqueurs bouncing in their hands, they bravely attempted to fraternize and have a party. We sneaked off to bed.

As we reached our swaying carriage, we found Geoff, our steward, stoking a small boiler with coal for the hot water and heating. Everything in the carriage, built in 1927, is original. It is truly a piece of living, working history, which is what makes it so

The Orient Express

special. In our absence, our compartment had been transformed into a deliciously cosy bedroom. The blinds were drawn, there was a tapestry-covered ladder to the top bunk, the lovely marquetry gleamed in the lamplight. We would rather be in this private haven, rattling through the night, than anywhere. The strange noises which steal into our sleep, the whooshes and whistles, the clanks and rattles and station tannoys, only serve to heighten the mystery and deepen the sense of security in the compartment. And where will we be when we wake up?

Switzerland is the answer. Ridiculously pretty, bright green meadows fringing a towering jumble of glistening white peaks. Breakfast comes with a polite knock: coffee, fruit salad, croissants. We stretch our legs at Buchs, and again at St Anton, where we watch the electric engine being changed. An iron hook is all that connects it to the long line of royal blue carriages which snake behind. The air is refreshingly cold and clean.

We wish we were going all the way to Istanbul. We don't want to get off. The couple next door, two of the old dears first glimpsed at Victoria, almost don't. This, apparently, is their 60th journey since the Orient Express service recommenced under its present management in 1982. The couple on the other side don't seem quite so enamoured. She calls home on her mobile: "You don't get much sleep on this thing. It's very noisy and it moves all night long".

We lunch in the Dolomites. We descend from the mountains to the Venetian Plain. Verona, Padua....we are on the causeway....

We step down from the train and shake hands with Geoff. He was the star of the show, gentle, knowledgeable, a master of his craft. We collect our bags and walk out of the station - straight on to the Grand Canal.

The Orient Express London to Venice, or Venice to London costs £1,165 per person sharing a double cabin. A return ticket costs £1,690. The price is inclusive of meals, but not bar bills. The service runs from March to October. For further information, contact VSOE reservations in London, tel 0171 805 5100.

Index of hotel names

In this index hotels are arranged in order of the most distinctive part of their names. Very common prefixes such as 'Il' and 'La' are placed after the name. More descriptive words such as 'Castello', 'Locanda' and 'Villa' are included in the name.

Index of hotel names

Index of hotel names

Index of hotel names

Index of hotel locations

In this index hotels are arranged by the name of the city, town or village they are in or near. Hotels located in a very small village may be indexed under a larger place nearby. An index by hotel name precedes this one.

Index of hotel locations

Index of hotel locations

Index of hotel locations

Special offers

Buy your **Charming Small Hotel Guide** by post directly from the publisher and you'll get a worthwhile discount. *

Titles available:	Retail price	Discount price
Austria	£9.99	**£8.50**
Britain & Ireland	£9.99	**£8.50**
USA: Florida	£9.99	**£8.50**
France	£9.99	**£8.50**
France: *Bed & Breakfast*	£8.99	**£7.50**
Germany	£8.99	**£7.50**
Italy	£9.99	**£8.50**
USA: New England	£8.99	**£7.50**
Paris	£8.99	**£7.50**
Southern France	£9.99	**£8.50**
Spain	£8.99	**£7.50**
Switzerland	£7.99	**£6.50**
Tuscany & Umbria	£9.99	**£8.50**

Please send your order to:

Book Sales,

Duncan Petersen Publishing Ltd,

31 Ceylon Road, London W14 OPY

enclosing: 1) the title you require and number of copies

2) your name and address

3) your cheque made out to:

Duncan Petersen Publishing Ltd

*Offer applies to this edition and to UK only.

Special offers

If you like *Charming Small Hotel Guides* you'll also enjoy Duncan Petersen's *Versatile Guides/Travel Planner & Guides*: outstanding all-purpose travel guides written by authors, not by committee.

Titles available:	Retail price	Discount price
Australia *Travel Planner & Guide*	£12.99	**£10.50**
California *The Versatile Guide*	£12.99	**£10.50**
Central Italy *The Versatile Guide*	£12.99	**£10.50**
England & Wales *Walks Planner & Guide*	£12.99	**£10.50**
Florida *Travel Planner & Guide*	£12.99	**£10.50**
France *Travel Planner & Guide*	£12.99	**£10.50**
Greece *The Versatile Guide*	£12.99	**£10.50**
Italy *Travel Planner & Guide*	£12.99	**£10.50**
Spain *The Versatile Guide*	£12.99	**£10.50**
Thailand *The Versatile Guide*	£12.99	**£10.50**
Turkey *The Versatile Guide*	£12.99	**£10.50**

Travelling by car? Duncan Petersen's **Backroads driving guides** include original routes and tours – avoid the motorways and main roads and explore the real country. Full colour easy to read mapping; recommended restaurants and local specialities; practical advice on where to stop, visit and picnic.

Titles available:	Retail price	Discount price
Britain on Backroads	£9.99	**£8.50**
France on Backroads	£9.99	**£8.50**
Italy on Backroads	£9.99	**£8.50**
Spain on Backroads	£9.99	**£8.50**

Please send your order to:

Book Sales,

Duncan Petersen Publishing Ltd,

31 Ceylon Road, London W14 OPY

enclosing: 1) the title you require and number of copies

2) your name and address

3) your cheque made out to:

Duncan Petersen Publishing Ltd

*Offer applies applies to this edition and to UK only.